# GOSSIP

# GOSSIP

## How to Get It Before It Gets You, and Other Suggestions for Social Survival

BLYTHE HOLBROOKE

ST. MARTIN'S PRESS : NEW YORK

GOSSIP: HOW TO GET IT BEFORE IT GETS YOU, AND OTHER SUGGESTIONS FOR SOCIAL SURVIVAL. Copyright © 1983 by Blythe Holbrooke. All rights reserved. Printed in the United States of America. No part of this book may be used or reproduced in any manner whatsoever without written permission except in the case of brief quotations embodied in critical articles or reviews. For information, address St. Martin's Press, 175 Fifth Avenue, New York, N.Y. 10010.

Design by Mina Greenstein

Library of Congress Cataloging in Publication Data

Holbrook, Blythe.
   Gossip : how to get it before it gets you, and other suggestions for social survival.

   1. Gossip.   I. Title.
HM263.H577   1983      302.2'24     83-9759
ISBN 0-312-34076-1

First Edition
10 9 8 7 6 5 4 3 2 1

# Contents

Introduction ix

### PART ONE
## Beginner / Presentation of Self

1. A Few Words About Gossip 3
2. When It's Good to Be Talked About (And When It's Not!) 9

### PART TWO
## Novice / One on One

3. In Confidence 19
4. Lovers and Other Dangers 26

### PART THREE
## Intermediate / The Pleasure of Your Company

5. Get a Grip on the Office Grapevine 33
6. Players 38

| | |
|---|---:|
| 7. The Dishonest Broker | *44* |
| 8. Boss Talk | *51* |
| 9. The Elements of Style | *58* |
| 10. Speculation | *67* |

PART FOUR

# Advanced / The Circle Game—Social Work

| | |
|---|---:|
| 11. Haute Biche Is Back! | *83* |
| 12. The Hostess Gets the Mostest | *92* |
| 13. Get Ahead as a Guest: Some Cocktail Strategies Explained | *102* |
| 14. Small Talk Is No Slight Art | *108* |
| 15. Who Wants to Hear What | *117* |
| 16. Psyching Out Social Gossip | *132* |

PART FIVE

# Expert / Hard-Core Gossip Gamesmanship (Handle with Care)

| | |
|---|---:|
| 17. Ask and It Shall Be Given | *143* |
| 18. Seek and Ye Shall Find | *154* |
| 19. Drive Defensively in the Fast Lane | *162* |
| 20. Preemptive Tattling | *178* |
| 21. When It's Already Out | *188* |
| 22. Character Assassination Explained: Or, How to Get Someone with Gossip | *196* |
| 23. The Whole Truth and Several Useful Variations | *216* |
| 24. Surviving a Bad Story | *222* |

*We live amid surfaces, and the true art is to skate well on them.*

EMERSON, "Experience"

# INTRODUCTION
# Getting into Gossip: The Story Behind the Stories

GOSSIP.

It fascinates us. It repels us. It informs, unnerves, entertains, and binds us. It offers vital intelligence, yet we disparage and make light of it. What makes a story "hot"? What makes it believable? Does gossip just grow crazily like cancer cells, or is it a code that can be broken and mastered? "What in God's name," I wondered, "is this thing called *gossip?*"

The more I thought about it, the less I was concerned with the "substance" of the stories I followed and the more I became interested in how one subset of lies, leaks, and speculation establishes itself as the "real" story. (Those of us in the news business usually take a schizoid view—checking and rechecking *until* an item is picked up by a competitor.) Although it's comforting to exaggerate the line between "hard" news and "speculation," we're rarely on such *terra firma* as we think. While what's fit to print is clearly important, don't sneer at the scuttlebutt, as it may prove even more critical.

Or so I learned. And so should you. This guide will enable you to profit from the observations of more than a hundred Most Knowledgeable Others. For, while through birth, brains, beauty, beastliness, love, or luck we may be privy to the scoop on certain state secrets, "star" wars, style shifts and inside-trading scandals, and while (with a little help from our dear friends) we can cast a net from Seoul to Sydney—*however* hyper we may be and however well-placed our sources, one man (even one woman) simply cannot keep *all* bases covered. "Inside" is ultimately not so much a place as a sharp approach to whatever nut needs cracking.

So *Gossip* grew and what started as a personal odyssey picked up speed as a social survey. Having earned my purple heart in the World's Capital, I shuttled up to the Big Apple where I spent several months closeted with the biggest, smartest, fastest, meanest mouths I know. From there, it was Hollywood, where I found the natives far less primitive than we Easterners imagine. Tireless, I questioned the authentic voices of snobbism, dynamism, money, pomp, politics, circumstance, stylish influence, and sheer brute power—asking them not to spill their secrets (nothing's staler than old stories) but rather to share their insights into the rules of the gossip game. (First rule: There's no better way to get the latest than by specifically *not* asking for it.)

I tracked down and chatted up promoters, hostesses, magnates, politicians, producers, secretaries, drag queens, critics, spies, investment bankers, corporate treasurers, entrepreneurs, lawyers, legislators, agents, academics, hairdressers, headhunters, lobbyists, and political organizers. I hit on writers, editors, art dealers, diplomats, maids, social secretaries, reporters, infamous gossips, social scribblers, fashion arbiters, packagers, dealers, masters of divinity, network whizzes, well-placed wives, high-priced maître d's, overpriced madams, casting directors, and former cabinet members. I even took a memo or two from management. This book is dedicated to the scores who shared their secrets—and who would absolutely kill me, should I name them!

# PART ONE
# BEGINNER

# Presentation of Self

# 1 · A Few Words About Gossip

> 'Tis no slight task to write on common things.
> 
> HORACE

No MAN is an island. Irredeemably social, interdependent, and oh-so-needingly intertwined, we're rather more like a colony of apes. Getting the signals is basic to survival, and the informal signals are most important of all.

If you want to be president, prima ballerina, tenured professor, or simply the next to move from gofer to administrative assistant, you have to know what's happening and keep an ear to what's coming up. Gossip* is the game of getting on top by looking ahead and staying in touch.

Everything happens first as gossip. Inside gossip, whether in Washington, Wall Street, or L.A., is always more accurate and informative than the "news" it eventually spawns. The way the world really works is set down in gossip. Gossip is the other tree of life, with frighteningly potent knowledge of good and evil. Small wonder many approach it with the same ignorance and hypocrisy that once characterized attitudes toward sex. Gossip is the last taboo.

"In the beginning was the Word," we are told. And no sooner

---

*For the purposes of this guide, "gossip" is unofficial information that, true or false, takes on a life and power of its own.

was man created than he began to gossip. Ancient references to gossip and gossiping abound. The likes of Seneca and Hesiod explored what the latter called "that most knowing of persons—gossip," and dramatists from Aristophanes to Stoppard have found gossips the ideal *dramatis personae* for keeping and dispensing secrets. While we tend to think of the gossip as a stock character, characters given to gossip run the range. Jane Austen's Emma was a gossip; Marlowe told, Richard II listened; *Wuthering Heights* is a housekeeper's tale of a stormy night; and Balzac's young Rastignac couldn't hear enough.

What were Dr. Johnson's *Tattler* pieces but gossipy notes? Journalism began as gossip, and much of it still is. Biography is gossip. (Boswell himself commends his *Life of Johnson* to gossip-lovers.) And history, revised or standard edition, is little else. Madame de Staël gossiped about Josephine, who gossiped about Napoleon, who gossiped about Josephine and Mme. Récamier, who gossiped about Talleyrand, who gossiped about everyone, and, more important, who knew enough about getting and evaluating gossip to serve and survive an emperor, a revolution, and a king.

While the uninitiated may believe that, like farm wives over the back fence, we merely gossip to pass the time, for us the medium is not the message. Gossip can have a positively earth-shaking impact. What was Deep Throat whispering to Woodward and Bernstein but office gossip of the most ear-to-keyhole sort? What squashed Teddy Kennedy's White House prospects? Not what actually happened at Chappaquiddick, but the endless rumors arising from the sloppy way he handled his news.

But gossip is important not only because of its impact on history. Every day, gossip plays a central role in each of our lives, expressing and fulfilling an even wider range of needs than our lovemaking. Listen closely to someone's gossip and you can pick up on his values, interests, insecurities, I.Q., income, and other vital information.

We gossip to get someone's attention, to build our ego, or to get news in return. We fight, flirt, get even, promote, and establish ourselves through gossip. We advertise our friends' successes and our enemies' failures. We gossip to amuse and entertain—to be thought clever and well informed—sometimes (often!) even telling more than we should, simply to be invited back. Gossip is one of the few remaining oral gratifications that is not immoral, fattening, or carcinogenic.

"What's happening?" we ask. "How's it going?" "How are you?" "How's business?" "How's Jane—has she found another job?" "What do you hear from Pete?" Dispatches from the inner circle feed our sense of "being there." And being there—alive, involved, and in the know—is what it's all about. True or untrue, gossip has an undeniable life and power of its own. The only absolute is that none of us is immune. Our choice is not whether we will be touched by gossip, but whether we will be its brokers or its victims.

While gossip can be a leisure activity, it is also central to most work situations. People gossip to keep up on business, to identify themselves with power people, to assert their status, and to impress others with the people they know ("Then Yoko dropped by after the performance . . .").

A commanding knowledge of gossip and gossips gives you the edge in conversation and helps keep you clear of potentially damaging situations at work. (Ever criticize a careless employee only to find that she was the boss's mistress, and yourself reassigned to left field?) Neither money nor fame nor the size of your power base can fully shelter you from gossip's fallout. A hundred-million-dollar merger of Phillips Petroleum and Crown Zellerbach was squashed by vague rumors that Washington wouldn't approve—before the appropriate agencies had even started considering it! Writer Ring Lardner, Jr. and radio personality John Henry Faulk were among the thousands whose careers were damaged by the late Senator Joseph McCarthy's loathsome trial by rumor.

Gossip can initiate powerful self-fulfilling prophecies. Rumor has it that movie magnate Joe Cohn's widow, Joan, divorced Laurence Harvey, her second husband, not so much for his alleged infidelities as to silence the humiliating talk. And who has enough spare talent to survive the killing phrase, "He's losing his touch?" Once *that* word is out, even seasoned pros have found it near impossible to get backing.

But gossip also has its up side. Many low-budget businesses and movies have nevertheless succeeded through "word of mouth," and many a career has been made by the simple rumor, "She's hot." Successful negotiating frequently depends on veiling one's real options and intentions in a confusing haze of conflicting news. The agent skilled at spreading stories of his client's popularity earns his fat commission. The fortunes of agents, publicists, politicians, performers—even pinstriped lawyers and chief executives—can be built or destroyed by gossip, which plays God to mergers as well as marriages.

The word *gossip* comes from the Old English *godsib* (*god* meaning good, *sib* meaning akin or related to). Indeed, the first meaning the Oxford English Dictionary gives the word is "sponsor to person baptized." Even the second definition is simply "a familiar acquaintance, friend, chum." It is not until the third definition, "persons, mostly women, of light and trilling character, esp. one who delights in idle talk, newsmonger, tattler," that we come upon society's working definition of the word. That definition is negative—such slander!

Like sex, marriage, and manners, gossip has always been the subject of jokes, but serious condemnation of gossip seems to have sprung from the more moralistic sects of early Protestantism. While the Catholic hierarchy was a hotbed of gossips kept in practice with frequent confession, Protestants were encouraged to keep their sins to themselves. Idle talk was considered so sinful that some of the early colonies actually outlawed and arrested gossips. Clearly, one benefit the authorities derived from this sanction, then as now, was to make *you* feel guilty for merely reporting what *they* did.

Much criticism of gossip is still simply hypocrisy, as Saki (England's up-market answer to O'Henry) observed: "Hating anything in the way of ill-natured gossip ourselves, we are always grateful to those who do it for us, and do it well." But while gossip is attacked as negative, the rumors flying on any given day are often much happier and more productive than the staples of riot, rape, and pillage offered us by the news media. Others avoid gossip because they have reached the astonishingly naive conclusion that if they don't talk, they won't be talked about. But "do unto others" is about as applicable to gossip as to adultery. The truth is people will talk about what others want to hear, and they'll talk about you if you're a hot topic. Accepting this inevitable is the first step toward getting control of the gossip that is out on you.

Is gossip's bad name deserved? The author of this entertainment thinks not. Of course, just as there are all kinds of gossips, so there are all kinds of gossip. Some gossip is essential, educational, and entertaining, while other kinds are vicious, ill-advised, or merely passé. Gossip is shallow or profound, "in" or for the masses; a tool for snaring money, fame, and power or a study in character.

Some see gossip as a black craft to be avoided, but there is no getting away from it. (There is only getting the better of it—or being gotten by it!) The wise man keeps this Ariel at his service. Whether one wades into the fray or retreats, one must keep up. John Locke was right: "The only fence against the world is a thorough knowledge of it."

This knowledge is best acquired in five stages. The *Beginner* who wants to learn how word of mouth works should first get a clear sense of what gossip is. Such basic training should also include advice on when it's good to be talked about and how best to position oneself to encourage (or discourage) gossip. Having mastered this, the *Novice* is ready to tell (or not to tell) his story one on one. Next, the *Intermediate* player learns to get a grip on the office grapevine and is given a useful guide to the gossip habits of his peers.

If the reader achieves only Intermediate-level skills, he won't have done badly. Still, the more ambitious among you might crave some small helping of fame, fortune, and, yes, even social acceptance, in addition to the usual double dose of wealth and power. So in the fourth, *Advanced* stage, we'll become "terribly social" and play the circle game—teaching you a range of cocktail strategies that will enable you to work the room like a pro or "hear it all" without budging from the comfort of your home. Advanced will also offer invaluable pointers on small talk—no slight art!

Last—and morally least—comes *Hard-Core Gossip Gamesmanship*. While these Expert techniques may be too hot for most of you to handle, it's best to be thoroughly briefed. To be forewarned, as they say, is to be forearmed.

Ready? Sound easy? Don't be too sure. Not for nothing did Spinoza note that "men govern nothing with more difficulty than their tongues and can moderate their desires more than their words." It is gossip, not love, that makes the world go 'round. If you don't know gossip's ins and outs, uses and abuses, dangers and delights, king- and pawn-making power, you are placing yourself at a severe and foolish disadvantage. So take your rightful place among the heads of state, power brokers, media people, politicians, executives, celebrities, socialites, administrative assistants, and all the others who trade in, thrive on, and succeed with the help of gossip!

# 2 · When It's Good to Be Talked About (And When It's Not!)

Modesty is not a virtue; it is useful only as a curb to youthful indiscretion.
ARISTOTLE, *Nicomachean Ethics*

WE'RE far from rational about gossip. Some of the best practitioners are the worst analysts. Much like the customs inspector who, when asked whether he took bribes, sputtered, "How dare you!" but when simply handed $1000, waved the offender through with a tip of his hat, we imagine that as long as we don't name the deed we're not really doing it. Similarly, most of us block the dreaded thought that we might figure in friends' talk, while paranoids imagine that others speak of no one *but* them!

Do people really talk about us? The answer is yes, of course. Ex's, enemies, lovers, perfect strangers, mere acquaintances, and, yes, even our dearest buddies—all have their say. After all, curiosity bespeaks affection as well as ill will. Imagine how boring reunions would be if we couldn't trade news on still-absent friends and family!

So why the big taboo on talk? Why can't we hear even a good friend's smiling, "Oh, we were just discussing you," without experiencing a slight shiver? Why do many sophisticated—even famous—people grow positively frenzied at the thought that they've been the subject of speculation—good, bad, or indifferent?

"If people really knew what others said about them," Pascal

noted, "there would not be two friends left in the world." Not simply because so many trash their "friends" but also because we're so incredibly touchy about what others are saying. The same remark we might find funny said to our face is judged treason when told back to us as gossip.

It is *control* we are fighting for with each anxious "what is she saying about me?" Hearing the word out on us we sometimes feel as violated as the savage who's sure the explorer's camera has magically snatched his "spirit." Unreasonable, perhaps, but human.

"Carve your mask," the ancient Roman emperor Marcus Aurelius counseled. Even the stone-age tribes of Papua, New Guinea, excel at carving masks. While fire and flint sure came in handy against the elements, the mask was man's first tool of social survival. This mask is meant to influence our talk, for, as Machiavelli observed, "everyone can see, but few can feel." Part of man's extended mask is his life story.

But while ancient heroes of obscure origin could simply claim themselves descended from the gods, today's rising stars must gloss over (or exploit) the undeniable. Like many legends, Chanel created a character as well as a distinctive look, publicizing certain episodes and pushing others into the background. While everyone *knew* Chanel had started as a demimondaine, Chanel herself kept mum and banished those too curious about her early days. Awful? Hardly; any public actor has such an "image." The question is not whether the talk about you will feature a character even your own analyst wouldn't recognize, but rather how you can have a hand in fashioning this elusive character.

## Good Rep

It is fatal to look hungry. It makes people want to kick you.

GEORGE ORWELL, *Down and Out in London and Paris*

"Here, everything is a PR game. You build up an image and then you stick to it," says an entrepreneur who operates in New

York and Paris. "Image and gossip are so important here in New York because you have this enormous mass media which needs constantly to be fed *something*—good, bad—anything, as long as editors think it's interesting. And my colleagues here! I never cease to be stunned by the exaggerated, self-serving remarks that are common practice in American business. Here, people always say their competitor is 'in serious trouble' and their business is 'just fabulous'—right up to the very day that they go bankrupt!"

A "good" gossip-generating activity is to get out, see, and be seen. "That's why people spare no expense on status accessories and go out to all the lunches. It's all part of looking busy, successful, and *invited*," says one tall, dark, and handsome model turned successful account executive. "With a little luck you then *actually* become what at first you only *seemed*."

A high, highly social profile is especially helpful when it's rumored you're losing your looks, your job, or your lover. "There's a saying, 'He wore a mask and his face grew to fit it.' I know that's meant in the worst sort of way, but I think a mask is a wonderful life-saver," one socialite remarks, eyeing her nails. "I remember running into a friend who'd been unemployed for three months. She looked so fantastic I just had to ask her how she managed it. 'You see, everything is so bad right now, I haven't the nerve *not* to look wonderful,' she said. And because she didn't fall apart, she's back, better than ever. Sometimes when you don't feel like going out, you should still get it together and go out—lest you be counted out!" Even if some guess your distress, you still win points for hanging in there.

"I was over at The Underground," said a gay friend, "when who puts the move on me but Nureyev. It was right after that *New York Times* magazine 'Time Catches Up with Rudi' piece. So we're dancing up a storm and I say, 'The *Times* is wrong about you; you have a lot of stamina.' 'Yes,' he says, 'and I have a lot of stamina in other places too!' " my friend recalls, aping a Russian accent. *Un peu risqué,* perhaps, but Nureyev knew what he was doing. Within hours the stamina story had supplanted the *Times'* inspired talk of the "how sad Rudi has lost it" sort—at least on the club circuit.

No doubt about it: endurance counts. (If you're going through some rocky times, you really have to make the scene.)

Most people steer clear of publicly trashing someone they know they're going to see at dinner.

Kissinger is the perfect example. When at his peak, he established himself as *the* chic invitation. "This helped him ride out a lot of turbulence," one powerful hostess explains. "Not to mention———," she smiles, naming one Wall Street wizard with a past. "God knows he's pulled some shabby deals, but why mention it when he's so brilliant, charming—and always just around the next corner!" A high profile gives you more say in setting "your" gossip agenda.

"That was one of Fred Silverman's *many* mistakes. The gossip columnists wouldn't have had to harp on what a white-sock-wearing klutz he was if he'd ever made the effort to do amusing things they *could* write about instead," one former Silverman colleague sagely suggests. If you're hot, people will talk—no matter what. Better make sure you feed them *good* news—lest others satisfy their curiosity with something far less flattering.

"Never let worrying what people will say make you stay at home unless when you do go out you show up, well . . ." says one wicked gossip, pausing and rolling her eyes for effect before launching into the "real sad" case of a "dear friend" and fellow blonde-about-town who, when she hadn't the courage to face her friends sober, took to belting down a few by herself *before* and showing up at parties "pre-plastered."

Moral? Never let hard talk keep you at home unless you've misplaced your mask. Every party loves a live wire—but if you're laughing all the way, smart folks in a sober town get suspicious.

Remember, bland can be beautiful. Ninety-eight percent of those working hard at keeping a high profile are still trying to blend in. That is why, should you say anything even moderately controversial, your "heresy" will soon be on all lips. How *not* to be hot? Mind your business and conduct your public life in the most pleasant and boring manner possible.

## When It's Good to Be Talked About

> There is only one thing in the world worse than being talked about, and that is *not* being talked about.
>
> OSCAR WILDE, *The Picture of Dorian Gray*

It's good to be talked about:

- When you're so hot it's pure adulation (you've just had a big success—or at least people imagine you have)
- When you've got something to sell, be it a book, paintings, clothes—or your sweet, sleek self
- When you're making a comeback
- When you're doing something interesting that "broadens" you (even a little "suffering" isn't bad if you're trying to shed a Mary Poppins image)
- When you want it thought you're being considered for a job or promotion
- When you want to create momentum as a "comer" or cash in (à la Ted Turner) on your image as a hard-driving maverick
- In short, almost anytime you're not dodging federal agents or mob killers.

"Fame is not fastidious about the lips which spread it. A celebrity collects a chorus of voices. All he wants is to hear them repeat his name." Thus notes Elias Canetti in *Crowds and Power*. But like all great "acts," celebrity is a marriage of craft and compulsion. Those headlines and glossy pictures aren't *just* a quick narcissistic fix. Celebrity is something you can bank on. One influential society editor explains it: "Look at Jackie. She courts the talk because that's her draw. Marrying her is like picking up the Hope Diamond—from a distance at least, the price seems offset by all the free publicity. People always talk about 'bad' gossip, but 'good' gossip does you far more good than 'bad' gossip ever harms you." Whether seeking fat endorsement fees, a new job, bigger markets, or a rich prenuptial contract, one is often well-positioned on the tip of every tongue.

## Succès de Scandale: *Black Is Beautiful*

> At the end of April, Noel Coward's *Fallen Angels* opened at the Hope Theatre with husky-voiced Tallulah Bankhead in one of the leading roles. The play was immediately described as "vulgar, obscene and degenerate" and became the talk of London.
>
> A. BARROW, *Gossip*

Sometimes, the first step is making an entrance—*any entrance*—and becoming "somebody." Helga Orfilla, wife of the Organization of American States ambassador, achieved capital fame overnight merely by showing up and sitting next to President Carter at a nationally televised ceremony—in a dress slit to her naval. While tackiness often nabs the limelight, even talk of downright awful behavior is rarely damning. In fact, a man's vices aren't overlooked; his failings fuel his rise more often than do his talents. While those who play Caesar's wife must shun the slightest taint, admitted rogues can get away with murder.

"You'd better watch out. *I've heard about you!*" one associate threatened an unabashedly black prince.

"Oh, God, what are you going to do? Ruin my reputation?" the merry amoralist shot back laughing.

Why does the whiff of scandal often advance a career? Convenience and complicity go along, get along. Those with the means to buy tend to like what can be bought. And then, as others say, "No surprises." One knows where the venal man stands. The "bad" won't shirk the dirty work or blow the whistle on Murder in the Cathedral. In fact, if you're looking a little too squeaky-clean you might float a rumor or two on yourself as vaccine against a full-blown scandal later; that way *you* get to choose your flaws.

But remember, don't tease when "owning up." Never bring a hot topic up just to play it down unless you actually intend to pique interest. Prince Egon von Furstenburg's confession to *People* that he had "experimented" with male partners horrified some straights while prompting sneers from swingers. But speaking of teases, should you hope to remain a long-running *succès de scandale*, keep your mouth shut! While a sly lyric is fine, nothing puts the fans to sleep faster than fully and frankly owning up.

Observe time and tide in all things. While it's generally good to see and be seen, don't overexpose. Although even Jackie O still hustles her queenly act, "Jackie's just like all the smart ones," one social pro observes. "She disappears for a while, and then she's suddenly back *everywhere* [with her social secretary calling ahead to alert the social pages]." While real recluses are rare, it pays to be thought a "very private"—read *exclusive*—person.

# PART TWO
# NOVICE

# One on One

# 3·In Confidence

> The greatest and most important things in the world are founded on weakness. This is a remarkably sure foundation, for nothing is surer than that people will be weak.
>
> PASCAL, *Pensées*

No, cynicism is not *everything*—but it is undoubtedly the safest and soundest thing! Best not to harbor grand illusions about man's character. Still, over the years you may make several true friends. Don't let the bad apples put you off, but do beware as you go sifting through the barrel.

## Scylla and Charybdis: *Between the Frozen Mask and the Nervous Breakdown*

> *Geraldine:* Have you given a thought to my predicament?
> *Dr. Prentice:* No, I'm too obsessed with my own.
>
> JOE ORTON, "What the Butler Saw"

There are two wrong ways to relate. One is with an "I'm terrific, things are wonderful!" mask pulled on so tightly it's as false as a fresh facelift. At the other end of the spectrum is the equally offputting perpetual breakdown. Steer clear of both. While it's often good to keep it light, pretend everything's *terrific* all the time and folks will start to wonder, "Who does he think he's kidding?" "What's he afraid of?" or "What's he taking?"

A good mood is, however, very important. Now that the straight-out sixties and self-centered seventies are, thank God, over, wallowing is no longer thought the *sine qua non* of "sensitivity." So remember, a friend is not a free psychiatrist. You should be patient with your friends—not be *their* patient. Get a grip on yourself and stop sniveling!

Which brings us to a rule. While there are times when confession is good for the soul (even good for friendship), show some restraint. A little goes a long way. Tell your story once; don't beat it to death. Keep it short, snappy, and concrete: plot, not pathology; story, not symptom. Remember, it's your life, not a case history; most couldn't care less for your "counter-cathexis."

## Let the Listener Beware!

It takes two to make a confession: the teller and the listener. Let's study the supporting player's role first. While it's generally safe to tune into second-hand blues, listening to the teller's own story can be dangerous. Letting someone tell you his sad tale puts you under certain obligations of friendship. A good rule of thumb: don't listen to the confessions of someone you don't already think you want to know better. We'll devote pages to "getting the gossip," but the real trick is *not* to let others get into the habit of telling you their problems!

If you encourage someone to pour out his heart (or merely neglect to discourage him) and then sit serene behind *your* mask, he may never forgive you. Coming clean is an old game with simple rules: I show you mine, you show me yours.

## Every Secret Thing

> Don't let young people confide in you their aspirations; when they drop them, they will drop you.
>
> L. P. SMITH

Sometimes our shyest secrets are so very shy that we never can quite face those with whom we have shared them. But smart gossips can see such fatal revelations coming: agitated pacings, chain smoking, meaningful pauses, and not-so-cryptic hints ("Remember last winter when Paula was away?") round out the effects that would get your friend booked on suspicion in any detective drama. Greet such stage business with a hearty "Shall we join the others?" Although that evening he may think you dense, at least the would-be secret sharer won't feel he must avoid you at work tomorrow.

You can also lose by letting others make foolish slips in more offhand ways. Jane ruefully recalls: "I once allowed a colleague to make a crack about a friend without even letting on I knew her. Later he saw us together—thick as thieves—and has avoided us both since." Moral? If they look bad, you look worse. Warn others off thin ice. Should a friend's name be mentioned in that naughty "here it comes" tone, flag your own loyalties before you let the speaker go one syllable further.

## Know Their Rules

"There are no secrets. We all have the same secret," insists a friend too bright to buy his own glib argument that there are no real differences between people. "We all die, don't we?" Yes, but so do plants, batteries, and giraffes. To recognize that essentially we all have the same secret is not to say there are no real secrets. A secret is an arbitrary thing. Your secrets are whichever real or imagined things you set apart and give a special place in your personal mythology.

It is no accident that legends from Oedipus on turn on riddles of identity, or that in folktales like *Rumpelstiltskin* the wizard's "secret" is none other than his true name. Our true identity is our first secret.

I don't care how much you're just dying to hear; before you let a friend even open her mouth, know how she expects you to treat her news. What stories does she consider most secret—professional or personal ones? Will she let you use your own discretion in briefing a mutual friend? Can you share all but one particularly sensitive item? Will she even accept some well-intentioned leakage on that? Or is even the fact that she takes tennis lessons classified?

"Information feels like love, and it feels like power," explains one journalist who says she feels betrayed when she hears even some of her more mundane confidances come back "reduced to anecdotes." She says she even felt "violated" when an acquaintance discussed a friend's tragedy—even though this news already had been carried by all three networks! Ridiculous? Maybe, but better know your friend's rules when you hear his true confessions.

## Let the Teller Beware: *Whom Can You Trust?*

> *Rosencrantz:* Good, my lord, what is your cause of distemper?
> You do surely bar the door upon your own
> liberty if you deny your griefs to your friend?
>
> SHAKESPEARE, *Hamlet,* III, 2

"A fool is his own informer," says the proverb, but in truth *Everyman* is his own informer. We can hardly help it. "The first object of desire is to be recognized by the others," Jacques Lacan writes. *Et voilà,* in our secret heart of hearts, we are all exhibitionists—up to a point. And so we often unload our griefs with overreaching hopes of love, peace, aid, comfort, support, and absolution; small wonder we often feel "betrayed" by those whose only sin was a failure to fulfill such great expectations. But alas, actual betrayal also abounds.

**Bad Bets** Anyone who, upon your second meeting, announces, "We're friends forever" is either a very sweet six-year-old, a cheat, or a hypocritical fool. Spare yourself the trauma of intimacy with either of the latter.

People who can keep your true confessions are not usually the kind who ask for them. We all hear rumors about our friends, but few are so insensitive as to ring up and ask flat out, "Tell me, is it true?" (Anyone in such a rush to get "the scoop" is no serious friend of yours.)

## Evasive Action

Someone is pressing you for news. Instead of snarling, "None of your business," try any of the following:

- *What's my line?* Have a pat answer ready to parry their indiscreet questions.
  Q: Why were you divorced?
  A: We both needed a wife.
- *Impenetrable opacity*
  Q: Is it true they're trying to ease you out?
  A: (calmly) Life and its rumors. What's this week's story?
- *Otherwise engaged*
  A: Let me call you back; I'm on the other line. (Then, just "forget" to return the call—or calls and leave a message.)
- *Stare them down* If they're dancing around a touchy item coolly call them out on it with questions of your own.
  They (after pregnant pause): . . . About the Congressman . . .
  You (with no particular interest): Why? What about the Congressman? Is there some problem?
- *The wrong true confession* If you're stuck together on a long flight to Tokyo and your associate is pressing hard for a confidence, *be* forthcoming: put him to sleep with tales of your Canadian childhood.

"It struck me recently that as long as I've known Tom (who you *know* is a compulsive talker), he's never told me anything *I could use*. He only gossips like *People* magazine—people you couldn't care about one minute," Jean sighs. "Or he will tell the inside deal on a shake-up at Paramount. Now there are plenty who'd give their ass to hear that, but he doesn't tell *them;* he tells me because he knows I won't remember! Or he talks about himself. He's one of those people who can go on about his shrinks, and pills, and complexes in a hysterically funny way by the hour. But news on people he needs for business—you can't get a *word* out of him!"

## A Time to Share

> A friend is a person with whom I may be sincere.
>
> EMERSON, "Friendship"

Caution can take you only so far. Obviously, you shouldn't burden your friends with all your problems, but there comes a time when it's a mistake for you *not* to share. "Putting a good face on it" is one thing; "putting on airs" is another. "The message on her machine says, 'I or my assistant will get back to you.' Can you beat that!" said a friend, referring to an acquaintance just fired. "I know she's not doing well, but how can I help her when she doesn't share?"

"Of course there are dangers," notes a thriving entertainment lawyer. "It can be risky to let others in on your plans, but sometimes it's more important to get the feedback or simply to build the bond. Sure, there's lots of sniping, but there are also people who've done business together for over thirty years without contracts. I keep some people's news tighter than I keep my own."

Another good reason to share: odds are nine out of ten "secrets" your friends will know already!

## Finding Your Trusted Few

> The wish for friendship develops rapidly, but friendship does not.
>
> ARISTOTLE, *Nicomachean Ethics*

A true and trustworthy friend is a rare prize indeed. "I think how close you are is determined by how far down the success ladder you meet," suggests one very Ivy League currency trader who swaps rumors with an international array of "friends," but who only shoots absolutely straight with a Morgan banker with whom he "prepped." While you needn't have grown up with someone to trust him, finding friends for all seasons generally takes a full turn of the good times–bad times cycle. While this can take years, in fast-paced sports like show biz and politics, what goes around, often comes around all too quickly. For there are friends and there are *friends*. Aristotle marks out three kinds in the *Nicomachean Ethics:*

> When people love each other on the grounds of utility it is motivated by their own good, and when they love each other on the grounds of pleasure, it is motivated by their own pleasure; that is, they love the other person not for what he is, but qua useful or pleasant. . . . Consequently, such friendships are easily dissolved. . . . Utility is an impermanent thing: it changes according to circumstances.

Wise Aristotle! "Utility is an impermanent thing" might stand as an epitaph for many a "good" friendship gone wrong. Choose your Trusted Few slowly, and guard them for a lifetime.

### Personals: *Delivering Your News to Selected Outsiders*

Sometimes during crisis we haven't the luxury of playing it close to the vest. How to tell mere acquaintances that you're getting divorced, being fired, or forced to sell the firm? Straight out and relaxed, always stressing the positive, "survival" aspect of your news. For example, "I don't know whether you've heard, but I left CBS for PBS. They're giving me a lot more freedom." (And a lot less money, but why mention it?)

# 4·Lovers and Other Dangers

Scratch a lover, find a foe.
DOROTHY PARKER, "Ballade of a Great Weariness"

SPARKS no sooner fly than the sex-flushed pair gets down to—er —talking. She offers a remembrance of flings past. He gets down on dishing his latest ladies. Such avowals would be bad enough if true. But part of what makes it fatal to be loved is no doubt that we *feel* it fatal and so we never sally forth sans armor. So look before you leap. Better make a few inquiries *before* you're bedazzled.

Arm in arm with our will to razzle-dazzle there persists an even fiercer will to lay it on the line with a perfect stranger. Just make sure that he or she is and remains a stranger. Don't be undone by detail. (Why have an unlisted number if you let Ma Bell plaster it all over your bedside extension?) But why chance it close to home at all? You don't speak Danish? Go to Denmark! You don't speak German? Then cruise Düsseldorf!

If you do slip up with local talent, just let it pass. Don't flag the indiscretion. If you say, "For God's sake, please don't tell anyone *that!*" your new playmate won't just tell *anyone:* he'll tell *everyone!* One experiment showed that children who had been *asked* not to play with a particular toy *didn't,* while the great majority of those who had been *severely threatened* . . . You guessed it!

"He said, 'You won't ever tell anyone will you?' and of course I swore I wouldn't. That's just not the sort of thing I'd ever say," a chum explains, grinning as she realizes that is precisely what she's doing!

## The Rotation Method

> Don Juan is the archetypal "man on the prowl," with his famous list of "a thousand and one"—that's practically the motto of the "dragueur." Their gossip always runs to lists— they're always trading information on their conquests.
>
> ROLAND BARTHES, (interview) *Le Grain de la Voix*

Some people are compulsively promiscuous, and most of these truly compulsive screw-arounds are carriers. No, I'm not just talking about rashes; they also spread half the town's undercover confidences. "Did you?" "Have you?" "Might you ever?" This sort has more questions than Nancy Friday. While I admit such characters are seductive, please remember to whom you're talking.

"But he tells me every secret thing!" you say. Yes, he tells everybody everything; he's pathologically free of "stranger anxiety!" His whole intimate revelations routine is like a cassette he pops in and reels off for "closeness." And for *this* you feel obliged to trade your secrets? More fun to put his routine on REJECT and ask him how the rest of the sorority answered the quiz you turned back empty.

"Unmarried men very rarely speak the truth about things that most nearly concern them; married men, never," says Samuel Butler—and he's a man, so he should know. But men and women do agree on one thing: men brag endlessly, far more than women, about their many lovers—or should we say *conquests?*

"There are few men who do not place felicity more in the opinion of the world on their being prosperous lovers, than in the blessings itself," Lord Halifax noted long ago. It's kiss and tell for sure, but slam the door in his face and you might still hear that you're headlining his list! Yet despite their own boasts, most men *think* women tell the truth about their sex lives, or, if anything, lie in omission. That's such a convenient thing to have them think, I won't betray my sisters!

*Do* women tell the truth about sex? Yes, I can confidently answer, most women do tell the whole truth and nothing but the truth—to just one, two, or three other women. But the trend is definitely toward the girls talking more like the boys. Now when a woman says, "Oh, you went out with him, what was he like?" she isn't asking if he's the sort who sends flowers!

Times have changed. The "girls" have changed. The things we say in bed may still be the same, but what we say to each other in the "right between the eyes" eighties is—well, all I can say is, if I were a man I'd be terrified!

## Love's Labour Lost: *Analysis Terminable and Interminable*

> The flux of language through which the subject tirelessly rehashes the effects of a wound or the consequences of an action. . . . I cannot keep from thinking, from speaking; no director is there to interrupt the interior movie I keep making of myself, someone to shout, CUT!
>
> BARTHES, *A Lover's Discourse*

Language is displaced desire. We get a certain rise out of telling, retelling, and yet again repeating our sad tale to the point of listener stupefaction. (But *we're* not bored. *We're* perversely enthralled. Why, this is even better than the thing itself!) CUT! Don't do this to yourself. Take it from me—he/she/it/they weren't worth making yourself more boring than a work-obsessed man or adoring mother.

Emotions are the ultimate luxury. We allow them at great cost and publicly avow them at a still higher price. Laugh and the world laughs with you; mope and, unless you're monied, you must mope alone.

"If you put people at their ease you eventually come out on top," one hardy social climber insists. "If they've abandoned you for a while, talked you down, you just glide past it, keep on smiling, and make them feel real comfortable when you *do* meet. And you know, people forget even their own gossip so quickly they may just do a total turnaround and say, 'We really like her.' "

We so value cool that there's a whole subgenre of true confessions that, while ostensibly about some event in the teller's past, are really about the *sangfroid* with which he is able to tell it.

## Dueling Scars

> My heart is broken but everything else is in working order.
> JOE ORTON, *Up Against It*

There remains a popular sort of tale that announces the teller knows the world for the horror it is, yet is tough enough to "take it"—and even more important, tough enough to tell it.

The icy coolest of true confessions, this anecdote à clef rolls trippingly off the tongue, wreaking a subtle vengeance at the same time it achieves a strangely worldly transcendence. (Why are such tales rarely told outside four-star surroundings? Does the sparkling crystal and glittering crowd help make light of the horror?) No matter. Like the Roman tribune who thrust his hand in the flame to show his captors that torture would be useless, we regale each other with tales of loss, survival, and disillusionment:

"Oh, that's nothing. You should be grateful that when he threw you out of the speeding car, at least he didn't back up to run over you. Did I ever tell you the funny story about the time my first husband Paul embezzled my last hundred thousand? It's a real killer—or at least *I* thought *I'd* die. Talk about young, s-t-u-p-i-d, and trusting!"

Such "and then they left me there to die" stories are masterfully all-purpose—in one stroke credentials, warning, and excuse: "Watch it, honey, I know how the game is played. Pull my punches? You kidding? After all, they did it to me, didn't they?"

# PART THREE
# INTERMEDIATE

## The Pleasure of Your Company

# 5. Get a Grip on the Office Grapevine

*If employees are so uninterested in their work that they do not engage in shoptalk, they are probably maladjusted.*
KEITH DAVIS, *Harvard Business Review*

---

A corporation is not a dinner party. Idle talk is out; information in. Even the best bits must seem serious. News, not entertainment, makes it with management.

But not all the news, by any means! While whatever sells goes in the marketplace, inside the company talk about one's colleagues had best be guarded: home team? or daggers-drawn medieval court? The marketplace may be a jungle, but a jungle at least affords some cover! Small wonder anxious executives officially frown on office gossip. Nowhere is the gossip taboo more stoutly maintained—or so obviously preposterous! Speak no evil, hear no evil—but get the jump. You're held a dangerous knave if you do—and a worthless fool if you don't—know the latest office gossip.

Communication is the corporate activity par excellence. There's no escaping the fact that for managers, minding your own business means monitoring everyone else's. Hour after hour, information flows up and decisions drip down. Yet much of the news on which decisions are based, even word of these decisions themselves, isn't official. Instead, preliminary market reports, personnel news, and political strategies are batted about the squash courts, dropped in the hall, or traded by the snackbar. In tense times, such talk becomes a potent subversive force. Swift and mighty flows the current of office gossip! While none can "control" the grapevine, understanding how it works *will* help you up the organization.

It's time to set some myths to rest. The grapevine can be a subtle, accurate, time- and face-saving boon to both manager and employee. (Yes, I said *accurate*.) While conventional wisdom urges that we scoff at what's in the wind, most studies show that the office grapevine gets it right more than eighty percent of the time (and scores in the high nineties on more mundane operational items). But while the grapevine often carries the truth, it rarely carries the *whole* truth. The trick is knowing what kind of news the grapevine tends to distort under what conditions.

How does the grapevine work?

Although "the grapevine" originally referred to news buzzing along a telegraph wire, gossip does not move in a single person-to-person chain (A tells B who tells C who then rings up D). Instead, one person, the "liaison," will pass the news to several others, with most of his listeners not repeating it (A himself tells B, C, and D—unless our liaison A happens to tell another liaison D, who then will himself *also* tell several others.)

Those whom psychologists call "liaisons" the world calls "gossips," "busybodies," or "well-informed" depending on their skill in handling gossip. While the "well-informed" are admired, the "busybody" is seen as a frustrated soul who'll say anything to win friends and bolster sagging feelings of self-importance. The difference? As always, exclusivity counts. Often it's less *how much* each type tells than the particular tale's appropriateness for its audience. Thus, while the well-informed source wins points for telling us what he thinks we'll enjoy hearing or especially need to know, the "busybody" loses our respect by telling absolutely *everything* to *everyone*.

Should you steer clear of such busybodies?

Certainly not! Whatever their official rank, such active gossips have a big hand in shaping office news. Cultivate the company gossip, but understand his bias. If a key liaison hates the head of finance, odds are this executive's prospects aren't half so dim as the talk has it. Is another liaison oversexed? Discount half the romance rumors from her section. Just heard half the department has a habit from the floor's biggest dealer? Remember, felony loves company. Better check his line out with a straight source before you buy it.

## Changing?

> The flying rumors gathr'd as they roll'd,
> Scarce any tale was sooner heard than told;
> And all who told it added something new,
> And all who heard it made enlargements too.
>   ALEX POPE, "The Temple of Fame"

We've all played "telegraph" at some point and heard how a simple sentence like "Mary had a little lamb," passed round the room, ends up "Marty hated lamb." Most of us assume rumors get similarly garbled. And it's true. Each teller automatically highlights some details and tones down others. Thus the story often shifts as each teller brings it into line with his world view.

Cognitive styles also come into play. While people who generally "repress" tend to level, shorten, and forget, introverts not only take in more of a story to start, they also "remember" still more details later! The news we remember and repeat is affected by everything from our self-esteem (the insecure talk more, but listen less) to the state of our stomach (tell them *during* lunch). We also "pick up" and remember more when sexually aroused—but not *too* very excited.

But when it comes to shoptalk, individual variables count less than the one big situational constant. Like faithful fans of some long-running soap, those in on the office grapevine agree on who's who and what's what. But like individual liaisons, office grapevines also have both strong and weak suits. Generally a first-rate reporter of power politics, the office grapevine's divining powers rarely extend to racier items. When the grand "passion" of the story is power lust, the office grapevine is a good reporter, but when the talk turns to sex at the top, it's far less likely to be accurate. Curiously, those few tales of corporate orgies I have on good authority were never reported. Who says company loyalty doesn't still exist? (Stock options must also argue eloquently for silence.) But while the board keeps word of stock-affecting scandals to itself, "human interest" stories that won't make the *Wall Street Journal* enliven the grapevine. Does Mrs. Waters drink a bit? Did Peter Samuels' temp spy a pair of silver high heels, size 11, in his bottom drawer just yesterday?

Some of the details may be off. Still, once rumors of someone's serious problems start circulating, the bottom line is clearly TROUBLE. If the tale is too "twisted," you can bet its hero will soon be leaving "to devote more time to family and personal business interests."

## Why Some Stories Spread Like Wildfire

What makes a story that may have shadowed you for years suddenly spring center stage and start the whole office buzzing? Clumsy handling can fan mere flare-ups into four-alarm blazes. A recent promotion, the rumor of a prospective one—anything that excites envy and interest—can add wings to old woes, as can the energies of witty enemies. But the most important element is timing. Flashfire rumors hit a nerve. Address preoccupations. When we know something's up, but don't know *what*, we'll grasp at any explanation. Uncertainty is the mother of invention. All flashfire rumors are attempts to answer the age-old question, "What just hit me?"—or "What is just about to hit me?" Indeed, far from some spoilers' plot, super-hot rumors are often essays in collective problem solving, with each new speaker passing on what seems to him most credible. (This screening leads some rumors to grow more, not less, accurate when flying among the cognoscenti.) But such happy progress is rare. As noted earlier, the office grapevine is amazingly accurate except when carrying emotionally charged news—the very stuff of flashfire rumors.

When a threat (of transfers, cuts, firings) hangs over the office, personal and official distinctions start to blur as all affected individual psyches merge into one anxious mind, its thousand eyes letting no potential clue escape unnoticed. (Whose file were the lawyers carrying? Did Mary arrive just after the chairman two mornings running?) But the same mood of expectant attention that fuels rumor's flight also fogs reason. We may see all sorts of clues but be too worked up to properly evaluate them. Expectations replace plausibility as the basis of selection.

When the gap between what one feels and what one has reason to feel is glaring, one experiences the uneasiness psychologists call "cognitive dissonance." Many a rumor springs from rationalizations spun to ease this discomfort. If, for example, the office is anxious about how the new boss will make cuts, people will tend to repeat stories that reflect these feelings ("I hear at the last job he sacked entire departments"). The whole story may have sprung full-blown from a headful of fancy, yet if it picks up on our own hopes and fears, we say it "sounds right." In times of crisis every man becomes a rumor-monger. Such rumors can also become self-fulfilling prophecies.

Still, even wildfire rumors ricocheting through the company tend to stray less than similar stories spreading through the world at large. (Witness the "Paul is dead" rumor so popular in the early seventies.) While masquerading as "news," such "star" rumors are more often a famished public's attempt to establish some shadowy (if pseudo) "inside" link to objects they can barely hope to glimpse, let alone know intimately. While all corporate intrigues are by no means played out in the open, sheer physical proximity keeps stories from straying too wide of the mark. No matter how large the corporation or secretive the management, you just can't, for instance, hide the serious illness of a top executive. (Even news on Hughes leaked out.) No man is a mystery to his secretary.

# 6·Players

"IN THE END it all comes down to people. This is a relationships business," Hollywood types are fond of saying. What's true of show biz is no less the fact at the company. The roles are just more structured. Each player has some gossip attitudes and options dictated by his job, while others reflect his personality.

Here is a brief, practical "Who's Who" for office gossip.

**Secretaries Aren't Stupid** *(And They Come in Several Very Different Varieties)*

Over the years the secretary has always been the office sleuth's first stop for inside gossip. (He was so clever, and she hadn't a clue what he was up to—or so he imagined.) While never so smooth a move as early office sleuths thought, changing times have made "pumping the secretary" positively misguided! However fey, tuned-out, laid-back, or sluggish she may appear, today's secretary is wise to the old tricks and should be handled very carefully.

**The best approach: her "good" side.** For the purposes of

gossip, secretaries come in five distinct varieties: temporary, angry, casual, career, and executive secretary.

**Approaching Tina Temp or Furious Flora.** These two are your best bets for information, and the only secretaries you should ever dare try pumping. The drawback with the temp is that she doesn't have much to tell. The danger with the angry secretary is that she may not only tell you what you want to know but also inform her boss that you were asking! (Not to *warn* him, but to *worry* him!) Since Furious Flora is likely not only to talk but to *tell* that she has talked, better steer clear—until you hear she's leaving. Then, by all means, buy her lunch to say good-bye—and hear everything!

While there are quite a few Furious Floras, by far the most common kind of secretary today is Easy Ella, the woman who isn't all that keen on being a secretary, but who hasn't yet decided what she might be keen on. This casual soul is loyal enough, smart enough, and, unfortunately, just friendly enough that you might imagine you could pump her. Don't try it! She'll be glad to give you the information you need, only so long as you don't alarm her by outright asking.

**Treat the secretary like the helpmate she is.** Tell her why you need to know. Appear forthcoming, ask her advice, but never push for information. Instead, present your problem, letting her find (and answer) the hidden questions. For example: "I need to talk to Dennis. Any hope for this morning?" you say, gingerly eyeing his half-closed door. (The less you pry, the safer you seem, and the more secretaries tend to help you.)

"I don't know," his secretary, Easy Ella, answers, which could have been the end of it, but you keep standing around as if agonizing over whether to wait or come back later. "They're in talking about promotion for the new show. He had me schedule the meeting for an hour, but it has been going on since 9:30," she finally volunteers, taking pity on your lonely vigil.

"OK, thanks," you say, "if he does come out before noon, you can reach me down the hall in Bernie's office."

"Oh, Bernie's in the meeting too," she replies, absent-mindedly reaching for her white-out, and you've got the news you really came for (but never would have gotten had you asked for it!).

While this seemingly direct approach works brilliantly with "casual" secretaries, don't try it on the careerists. They will see through your ploy and resent it more than a straightforward question.

**How to handle Career Chris.** She's the one who's not going to be a secretary too much longer if she can help it. The best and only way to get gossip from a secretary with a future is to let her know you think she's able. Get in there, promote her career, and expand your network while assisting the inevitable. Show an interest where it counts with her and rest assured, what she doesn't tell you hasn't happened.

**Miss Wylie, the executive secretary.** This is a far harder nut to crack. "Executive secretaries, they're the real yentas!" sighs an Easy Ella. It's hard to know what Miss Wylie thinks about that, 'cause whatever she thinks, she wouldn't tell you. (Hired by the boss straight out of Katharine Gibbs, class of '47, she has devoted her entire life to serving him.) Unless you remind Miss Wylie of a long-lost nephew, there is no way on earth you can get her to breathe one word beyond what she thinks is in her boss's interest. So where you can't possibly win, at least gain points for yielding gracefully. If you don't, Miss Wylie will not only block your ploys, she'll do all she can—rather a lot—to limit your access to her master.

**Don't try to establish rapport by swapping stories.** Of the many possible wrong approaches to Miss Wylie, the worst is affecting a false chumminess. (A thorough-going authoritarian, Miss Wylie can't bear to see even middle management stoop.) Since the only thing she respects is power, your best bet is to act like the "superior" you are and make inquiries through your secretary. ("Hello, I'm making a list of August sales for Mr. Bentson and I need to know . . .") You'll be astounded how forthcoming Wylie will be to questions posed through proper channels.

## No Margin for Error: *Defense*

**Your own secretary is both your first line of defense and an early-warning system.** If she's nice but indiscreet, pawn her off on an enemy. If you simply don't get along, fire her immediately—or suffer the awful consequences. (Only an indiscreet mate is better positioned to make you suffer!)

Your secretary should consider herself your special confidante—and *not* discuss your business with others. While she should feel free to ask you occasionally for news, you need not feel you *have* to answer. "Part of why we get along so well is that we're friends, but she knows there are limits," says one hip record executive whose secretary adores him. "The key is that she sees in me two things: both a friend who shares and a boss who might say, 'Sorry, I just can't talk about this.' I don't keep secrets for the sake of 'keeping secrets' from her," he explains. "If there's hot news the girls are bound to pick up, why shouldn't I let her know? She's smart. News she passes to Alice today may be repaid with a tip we need tomorrow."

**Recognize your secretary's great potential as a source; she's your liaison to the other girls.** Instead of making a fool of yourself trying to pump an opponent's secretary, send your secretary with clear instructions; she'll often do far better than you would have! But don't blame her if she comes back empty-handed. After all, his secretary may not know.

It seems secretaries just don't keep up like they used to: no doubt in part because the sort of woman who was yesterday's tuned-in secretary is today's up-to-date account executive. Legal secretaries, medical secretaries, and other specially trained paraprofessionals seem exempt from the general decline of secretaries as savvy yentas. But even when all the secretaries are just talking last night's made-for-TV movie, office news is still far from neglected. The following are a few more common office types. Recognize them?

**The Secret Sharer.** This is the classic liaison. At forty-nine, fifty-three, or thirty-seven she's office manager or head of traffic, but whatever her age and however far she has climbed, after a career of crisis management for the far-better paid, the Secret Sharer knows she's now as close to the top as she's ever going. Overworked and underemployed, she's both frustrated and bored —or at least she *was* before she started picking and promoting favorites.

What does this officially far-from-powerful lady have to give her candidates? After twenty years of fetching, carrying, coming early, staying late, and covering up for favorites, the Secret Sharer knows the company, its officers—their lives, wives, kids, mistresses, and drinking habits—as no one else does. Her secrets are everybody's secrets, and she'll share them all with promising newcomers for the asking—and the telling.

**Charlotte's Web.** While you should keep in touch with Secret Sharers still in the fray, steer clear of senior executives who didn't quite make the top spot and so are just making mischief until retirement. (While the Secret Sharer is still running the office for thirty thousand dollars a year, this one is lunching at La Côte Basque and pulling down one hundred thousand.) Witchy, bitchy, and racked by envy, Miss Charlotte knows she has no future and may try to make sure *you* also have none.

**Snow White.** Even the good can do you in. Remember those well-meaning, substance-oriented souls, the "dead-enders" who almost never pass it on? The perfect office confidants, right? Wrong! Snow White's innocence is also ignorance. While not "dangerous" in the same sense as those who slander with intent, those who "inadvertently" repeat your remarks in an unfortunate context do you just as much harm. Stick to your own kind, foxy! Let political naïfs hang others while learning the ropes.

**False Prophets.** Every office has one. The poor man plays Howard Cosell to office struggles and (unfortunately for those who bet his tips) always calls it wrong. Not surprising. Anyone who talks openly about office power struggles obviously doesn't know the score.

But while pros ignore his calls, new kids get taken in. "I had just taken a junior account spot in an ad agency and the senior executive on the account knew everything and everyone—or rather everything about everyone—or so it seemed. I would listen to him by the hour: who secretly hated whom, what were the hot affairs, who was just about to get fired. I just operated as if everything he said were fact—never once thought to check *him* out with someone. I remember thinking how lucky I was to be working with this guy, how lost I would have been without him. As it turned out, it was really just your classic case of the blind leading the blind!"

**Nervous Nellies.** These are people who should know better (who should *do* better), but who never make the final cuts because they always go to pieces in a crisis. Although Nelly's on-paper credentials seem fine, there are such gaping holes in her practical understanding of people and process that her stories lurch from shaky premise to unfounded conclusion. (Nonsexist notes: There are lots of Nervous Neds, too.)

Both Neds and Nellies should be avoided. Their company unnerves the wise and encourages the foolish. Worse, give them even half a minute's news and they'll race around the office spreading jumbled versions of *your* story.

**Chicken Littles.** These represent an even more extreme form of Nervous Nelly. Bearers of nothing but bad news, they imagine that they win friends and influence people, but they're only welcomed by the hopelessly paranoid.

**Organizers.** Give me a "doer" any day! While committees may not be your cup of tea, "joiners" do get around, make things happen, hear what's up—and what's more, they tend to get it right far more often than the excitable self-centered types described above. While not "gossips" in the pejorative sense or style, organizers have a wide range of contacts and a fair stock of authentic news they trade freely. Just be wary of Bud the budding pollster who asks (in confidence, you think), then features your answers in his announcements. We've all wanted to slip under the conference table when Bud begins, "Well, I know that Marty and a few others feel that . . ."

# 7·The Dishonest Broker

The World wants to be deceived.
SEBASTIAN BRANDT, *Ship of Fools*

WHILE one must learn how to handle Ned and Charlotte, for God's sake, don't take them as models. Far better to ape the lion or his foxy go-between, the "dishonest broker."

Most smart corporate gossips start off as staff assistants. You learn from the lion you tend. Even more important, a good staff job is a natural liaison position. Far from being censured, you are paid and promoted for shuttling back and forth between departments, meeting people, building networks, making inquiries, and sniffing out the inside stuff on people, problems, and process. You've not only got *carte blanche* to ask—those anxious to keep your boss's good will must answer.

## His Master's Voice?

> Any initiative from below can be halted by a mere hint that it will meet with disapproval "at the top"—No use asking who approved or disapproved.
>
> NADEZHDA MENDELSTAM, *Hope Against Hope*

Any staff job calls for hand holding. What's the world's best executive pacifier? Gossip! Big scandals, little insights, exemplary stories, and apocryphal tales are all grist for the mill. But boss talk isn't just hand holding. Remember the corporate motto, "No surprises"? Even the lowliest assistant-to had best brief his boss on all the news—before it happens. And briefing the boss is only half the job. Back and forth between the lion and his lieges our wily, wired dishonest broker dances. Each side expects his first loyalty. But is he really pawn of the powerful or an advocate of the people?

"Don't let them know I'm asking, but find out how they'd take to a big promotion for Peter," growls the lion.

"Don't tell him the deal's in trouble. Just say that we're still meeting," plead the troops.

What's a courier to do? Why, give your associates what they want. Act the dishonest broker they insist on having!

## The Go-Between

> One cannot both be sincere and seem so.
>
> ANDRÉ GIDE, *The Counterfeiters*

How to act the liaison without seeming the scheming pol, stool pigeon, or spy? While clearly calling for a master of finesse, the role of go-between admits a wide range of interpretations.

The two key variables: the corporate style and your boss's personality. Handling the first is simply a question of common sense. Most companies loathe rugged individualism in all but long-dead founding fathers. So work within the operational norm. Their best style is your best style. When in Rome—or at Morgan Guaranty or Benton & Bowles—gossip accordingly.

Psyching out your boss's personality can be trickier. Some insist on knowing everything, while others are equally adamant about their need *not* to be bothered. Both extremes breed their own type of disaster: paranoid bosses don't give their go-betweens enough room to breathe, while "above the fray" types give subordinates so much rope that even the naturally restrained can end up hanging themselves.

If you find yourself serving a paranoid, move on. Even in the best spots, satisfying the lion's appetite for news without turning the ranks into a camp armed against you is no small problem. Smart go-betweens know when *not* to answer their lion's bellow. For example: "Where is that report? I want to know why it's late and expect to see it on my desk tomorrow!" growls your lion.

"I'll find out, sir," you reply—already knowing, alas, that a very popular unit manager lost the damn thing (a firing offense) when he sent it out of house for typing. He confessed to you in tears; it could have happened to anyone. Only your competitor (who will snap him up) will be aided by his going. What to do? Race into the lion with your news, or cover for the unit and earn their eternal gratitude?

What did our foxy go-between say when the lion roared in the next morning? He said, "Excuse me, Leo, but this just came in," producing a wire reporting foul-ups by one of the fox's enemies. The readiness is all. With one loud roar, Leo was off and springing. When he finally strolled back into the office licking his chops just after lunch, the new report was waiting on his desk. "Just tell them I expect to see things more promptly in the future," Leo grunts, waving off what seems the start of Foxy's long and boring explanation.

Saved by a lucky wire? Hardly. That branch had been complaining for weeks and you'd promised to pass their news along when Leo was "in the mood for action." A quick call yesterday afternoon inspired the morning's wire, and the rest, as they say, went like clockwork. Foxy's great strength is not that he tells everything, but that his access allows him to leverage what he does tell for the maximum impact.

While you generally want to be the one who feeds your lion, if his mood or the news is too foul, call an ally and get your news recycled as a memo.

## Seeming Trust

But now I can just hear faithful lieutenants howling, "How could I mislead my mentor who tells me *everything!*" My only answer is, "Look again." If your mentor truly tells you everything, you've apprenticed yourself to a fool (who hasn't heard what sons do to fathers, and protégés to mentors!). Whole prides of lions have been bumped for foxy assistants offering the board twice the flexibility at half the salary.

**Mentor and protégé's best habit is in seeming trust.** There's a world of difference between telling everything and telling almost everything.

**Power from the people.** While you may feel as if your power filters down to you from the boss, much of your news and influence springs up from good relations with colleagues and underlings. Don't get cut off from the troops. Lose their trust and you've also lost your value to the lion. When in doubt over what to report, err on the side of shielding the troops, rather than playing the overzealous informer.

**He sees you when you're sleeping . . .** Though you should cover for the troops, don't let them get careless! Foster the myth of the omniscient lion. It takes the presumption of guilt (for ratting) off you if colleagues think nothing escapes the boss' notice. This myth also makes it easier to take the "since he's going to hear it anyway, you may as well let me tell him" tack when you need to break a confidence. And when you do manage to keep the beast at bay, your saves will seem all the more miraculous.

**Less than you know.** While playing up his master's omniscience, the smart go-between always plays down his own information for several very practical reasons. Most obviously, the smart aide has no desire to upstage his boss and incur the wrath of the lion-sized ego! (Feel free to drop in an occasional bit, but unless "briefing" is part of your official job description, never lecture.) Aides too often go wrong by gushing out inside gossip to let their lion know how "up on the latest" news they are; but instead, they only impress him with their indiscretion. Of course, if there's serious trouble where the lion isn't looking, you should let him know. *Very* carefully.

When talking with your boss you want to appear alert and well-informed, but in a deferential low-key way that never threatens the boss or makes him feel foolishly out of it. Above all, don't flaunt what you've got. The last thing you want to do is egg your lion on to tap competing sources. Remember, lions aren't shy. If your boss wants more news, he'll ask (or order!)

Downplaying the extent of your intelligence is equally important when dealing with the troops. Play "I know something you don't know" with your colleagues and they'll (quite understandably) hate you! They'll also clamor for news you aren't free to give them. Your best ploy is to act as if you barely know more than they do—if even that much! ("What do you mean, 'Are they really going to close the New York office?' What have you heard that makes you say that?") To make your protestations of ignorance more convincing, ask *them*. Incredible, perhaps, but so flattering, they may believe you.

### What Did You Know? When Did You Know It?

As Watergate defendants discovered, knowledge is also legal responsibility—yes, even for bits picked up off the office grapevine. Our three rules:

1. Don't nose around "locked closets."
2. Don't seem the scandal monger, and people won't offer you dangerous dirt.
3. If you *do* stumble upon indictable offenses, either report them to the prosecutor's office or keep absolutely quiet. Pass the news on to "just" a few close friends, and you're a thousand times more likely to get called up to tell your news again to the Grand Jury.

### One Word on Whistle Blowing: *Don't!*

Long-standing criminal practices do pay. Try to stop the malefactor and your case will probably never even get to court—but your career will certainly be ruined! If you don't like your boss's business, quit, or quit and tell—but don't imagine you can both cry "foul" *and* keep scampering up the corporate ladder.

## How Did You Like Working for Attila the Hun?

The appearance of loyalty is terribly important. While it's all right to smile at stories told by others, barring an open break, no aide enhances his standing by badmouthing his boss, however terrible.

## Source at the Top? Or, Who's Feeding Whom?

Consider the number of underlings always eager to offer the lion the choicest morsels, no doubt hoping, Cinderella-like, to attract the Prince's interest to their careers as well as to their story. But lions are rarely grateful for news. They assume *droit de seigneur* on all office gossip.

The lion will lend an ear, of course, and that attention alone is enough to keep most would-be confidential agents talking. Alas, the poor would-be agent often lets this illusory relationship with his "source at the top" go to his head, and instead of hiding his "connection," he flaunts it, implying, "You'd better be nice to me, or *else* the lion might hear." Needless to say, his immediate boss and colleagues soon exclude the snotty viper from their secret councils.

So his stories dry up. Soon he has nothing to tell his friend the lion who no longer receives him, instructing his secretary simply to ask whether there is anything "important" she should pass on instead. While the source saw himself as an important "listening post," the lion viewed him as just another bug: useful, like all bugs, only so long as he wasn't discovered.

## Training Your Lion

Of course, some really do have a source at the top. In such cases, train your lion not to leave his name when you're out. Nor should you position yourself as the young comer "in the know." A source at the top can be a great practical aid—but only if you keep it quiet!

What if your tie-in to the lion is quite regular and above-board (you're his staff aide), only he never tells you anything? How to get him to share more news? First, be sure to reinforce him for the things that he does tell you. Another good ploy: come in early, stay late. Even the tightest-lipped loosen their ties (and tongues) before and after hours. If he still doesn't share, call him on it. Calmly. Ask him if you've done something that has led him to hold you in less than full confidence. He may not even be aware of all that he's not sharing! Gently but firmly, make him aware.

Of course, don't just step into the job and expect your lion's trust. Close professional relationships take time (and tact) to develop. And he's never going to tell you *everything*. But if it hurts him to share even bits that might help you help him, start looking around. You need to find yourself another lion.

# 8·Boss Talk

*I wonder what the King is doing tonight?*
ALAN JAY LERNER, *Camelot*

---

LIONS love to be talked about. Lions hate to be talked about. Lions are inevitably talked about.

From the moment he roars in until the time he's brought down, the lion's moods, mind, and *modus operandi* chart the corporate course and determine each employee's trajectory. Small wonder that word of his every move is quickly passed from mouth to mouth and subjected to the knowing scrutiny of corporate sages. No tale is too small. No taste (whether for jellybeans or Apple terminals) too insignificant. What's up with the lion is what it's all about. There is no hotter office topic.

## The Sound of One Shoe Dropping

> The moment of *survival* is the moment of power. Horror at the sight of death turns into satisfaction that it is someone else who is dead. . . . [O]ne experiences a unique feeling of invulnerability. . . . "I am *better* than they are/I *survived*."
> ELIAS CANETTI, *Crowds and Power*

While not so hot as "wildfire," rumors of impending firings, failures, or foreclosures can cast a shroudlike pall over the victim's dealings for weeks, months, sometimes even years. Such rumors can slash sales, morale, and company credit—an element of self-fulfilling prophecy often accelerating the eventual collapse. The bigger the brass, the more debilitating death-rattle rumors are for the entire company. (Witness how a giant like NBC was nearly paralyzed as everyone from messenger to station manager waited for the axe to fall finally on "the man with the golden gut," Fred Silverman, whose luck had at last run out.)

Why can't we resist relating our lion's troubles even when it weakens our own position in the industry? (Of course, there are always the old scores to settle, but rarely *that* many.) Everyone in the industry knew Silverman was a goner for years, so why did "death of Freddie" stories still command an attentive audience? Quite simply, for the joy of sharing the happy fact that "he's a goner and we're not."

## The Man of a Thousand Masks

> All superior men need a mask.
>
> NIETZSCHE

The lion wants nothing more than that he *not* be understood. The lion's first love is control, and he knows he can't control the grapevine.

The lion can safeguard his secrets in many ways. The first and most obvious is through the use of masks. All powerful people develop an outer layer, "the me everybody knows"; that is their first level of contact. They create this image in part through skillful use of "signature stories": the modern corporate equivalent of George Washington's "I'll never tell a lie" cherry-tree tale, or JFK's "heroic" P.T. 109 fable—good schmaltzy stuff (often stressing fighting team spirit, style, and courage) that, like the best candid photos, catch the boss as he would like to be seen, whether or not that's his true nature! (There are also antihero archetype tales: young Hugh Hefner leaning over the kitchen table cropping nudes, or vintage Hef wrapped in blondes and smoking jacket.)

While a good "signature" goes a long way in shaping subsequent tales, bad stories can trip you up just as surely as Jerry Ford famous pratfalls.

## Secret Powers

> The gods never commit themselves—never stand to be questioned, no force can penetrate their intentions.
>
> ELIAS CANETTI, *Crowds and Power*

However nicely phrased, the corporate lion's question is command; his most casual-seeming query, forcible intrusion. After all, he's the boss. You can't simply refuse to answer. Yet while he can interrogate you, you dare not quiz him back. The famous "loneliness at the top" springs from the lion's own decision not to share his secrets. And a sound tactical choice it is! Power theorist Canetti goes so far as to define freedom as "the power not to have to answer a question."

What is the lion's premier secret? His will to survive at any cost: over your dead body, mine, that of his protégé, even the corporation. It's the secret at the heart of every other secret. The next layer? The means by which he will survive: habitual strategies, favorite tactics, and alliance networks. The still far from accessible surface? This week's top projects, pains, and plans. Most immediately, the challenge of safeguarding those secrets he must entrust to others for development and execution. How to get others to keep his secrets, especially those that might be prefaced with the status-enhancing tag "the boss just told me"? By far the most effective way is to make *your* secrets *their* secrets. Let confidantes know that you are counting on their discretion (and that should news leak, there will be consequences). Offering specific reasons why they shouldn't "tell" also helps. People may not be rational, but they like to think they are. Accountability (tell but a few and let them know that only *they* know) and good general morale also help ensure quiet. While some kind of talk is inevitable, the company always rife with rumor is ill-managed.

## Mixed Signals

Another approach to keeping secrets was practiced to perfection by that fox among lions, FDR. Few ever knew what he'd do next, not because he never told anyone what he was up to, but because he always told everyone his plans—in different versions!

"Ah, Roosevelt, he drove us crazy," sighs a former secretary of the air force and "kitchen cabinet" member. "First, he'd call one in and say, 'You have my full confidence to try this'; then he'd call another in and tell him *he* had his full support, sending him off in just the opposite direction! You never knew where you stood with him."

The troops can't revolt if kept constantly off balance.

## Gloom at the Top—Paranoid Isn't Powerful

> No administrator in his right mind would ever try to abolish the management grapevine. It is as permanent as humanity is and should be recognized, analyzed, and consciously used for better communications.
>
> KEITH DAVIS, "Management, Communication and the Grapevine,"
> *Harvard Business Review*

There are three types of lions when it comes to gossip: the winners, the survivors, and the losers. While there are a number of possibly winning techniques, most losing lions fall prey to the same flaw—their own excessive need to control even the grapevine.

"He wants you to know everything, but he also likes you not to know as much as he does," sighed one smart aide-de-camp, leaving her boss for a less nerve-wracking lion.

All lions are greedy, controlling, and famished for approval, but the losing lion no sooner extorts acceptance on one front than he's pushing for it on another. While the winning lion usually listens and "lets be," the losing lion roars over even innocuous bits. Result: The paranoid lion who wants to know everything yesterday—but can't take hearing anything—only gets the doctored news he merits.

## Rumor's Rules of Order

While the importance of rumored news is often what makes a story take off, certain less weighty subjects have such a hold on the corporate psyche that they may spread faster, stay longer, and in the end have far weightier implications than stories about what may be more "important" items. What makes for such compelling talk? The classic elements: a man, a woman (another man or woman), pride, arrogance, ambition, and that favorite sin of sins —overreaching. For, like even the earliest Greek dramas, classic corporate gossip is about limits; how far you can push it, and under what circumstances.

## Mary, Mary, Quite Contrary—*Or, How NOT to Handle a Rumor*

The story is simple. Boy meets girl. Boy hires girl. Boy promotes girl. Natives grow more and more restless watching girl's meteoric rise. Boy ignores grumbling on grapevine. Boy keeps promoting girl, elevating her to senior vice-president for development of his Fortune 500 company, just slightly over a year after first hiring her as his staff assistant. Restless employees grow mutinous. Grumbling not only grows louder, but items romantically linking Chairman Bill and blond protégé Mary are leaked to local papers. Finally reacting (wrongly) to the malicious barbs now flying like a hail of arrows, Chairman Bill denies rumors of romance at a public meeting—attended by the press—and turns his company affair into a national story to remember! (The ensuing acute corporate embarrassment forces Mary's resignation.)

What happened? While often elitist in subject, rumors are democratic in effect. Rumor gives power to people usually out of the decision-making loop. It's one of the few ways in which employees can warn the lion, "See here, you're going too far!" without suffering the dire consequences of outright telling him. Even boy wonders ignore persistent warnings at their own peril. (You can't fool all of the company much of the time.) Still, the chairman might have gotten away with it if he hadn't taken the loser's tack of not only forcing his team to swallow a bitter pill, but even refusing to let them grimace! Repression is the mother of dissension.

## How to Handle a Rumor

The losing lion tunes out what he doesn't want to hear, only to rage against "rumors" once it's too late. But the winner knows it's critical to surround himself with trusted go-betweens who keep him up on all the latest. This king of corporate beasts first floats a rumor; then uses formal channels to confirm this talk, only after evaluating grapevine reaction.

But even the best of lions sometimes comes in for a bad rumor. How to stop it? Studies show that "prompt, unequivocal disproof" is key. "Prompt" is doubly important, because rumor spreads most rapidly when fresh. You want to catch the story before too many repeat it (and so develop a personal stake in believing "their" story). This doesn't mean that *you* should instantly honor scurrilous stories with reply; just send your dishonest brokers out to laugh it off immediately.

But easy does it. Even hypocrisy has its limits! You needn't explicitly admit the obvious, just don't insult your colleagues' intelligence with a denial.

## Surveillance

While the lion's not wild for any "boss talk" he doesn't start himself, he is always poking his big nose into other people's business. In fact, the bigger your lion, the nosier, studies show. Top executives are more interested in learning "what's up" than lesser managers. They have more time for informal talk, and they take full advantage of it.

One can argue that it's easy for a lion to keep on top of things, since he quite literally *is* "on top," where news of hirings, firings, new projects, etc., most often originates. But lions also get the jump on news filtering up from the ranks. Studies show that stories that start way down the corporate ladder often skip over middle management and shoot straight to the top—only reaching those nearer the scene after filtering down from higher management!

# 9·The Elements of Style

> Everything is in the execution.
> NAPOLEON (reported in *Napoleon*, by Felix Markham)

MENTION the word *style* and the mind dances with visions of Wildean wit and haute biche banter. But such entertaining airs aren't for the office. "You're just desperately trying to get the true scoop from the most reliable sources and you don't give a damn *how* they tell it," says one great all-round gossip. She's overstating her case, though; we do care how shop talk is told.

While the best overall office style clearly "means business," one that is too brusque can be offputting. Our favorite office gossips are reassuringly low-key, competent-seeming, and ironically amusing.

## Creative Caution

Keep this checklist in mind and show creative caution:

1. *Don't appear to be a gossip.* Be interested, keep up, reinforce those who drop in to brief you. But don't push. Discretion is the better part of the corporate advancement our times think valorous.

2. *Don't dish the dirt with the rest of the girls.* Some female

executives go too far, avoiding all informal contact with secretaries (lest they be mistaken for one), but inappropriate familiarity can also breed contempt (and always produces gossip). While shop talk flows between all levels, true gab-fests are the magic glue that binds mentors and protégés, or coequal cronies. Don't effect familiarity with those too far above or below you on the corporate ladder.

3. *Invitation to a beheading.* Remember "Let them eat cake"? Don't lose your head. Save your *bon mots* for society. What's witty in one context can be fatal in another. At work, bland is beautiful. Avoid gossipy phrases like "You won't believe what I just heard!" with all but your closest cronies.

4. *Follies.* You can travel half the world on a business trip, but you can't escape the company's global reach. (If you're there doing business *now,* however remote the spot, colleagues and competitors will follow.) So watch it. Cruising the Hong Kong leather bars might get you roughed up back at headquarters!

5. *No trails, please!* While you're watching your talk don't get careless with physical evidence. ("For God's sake," advised a friend, "tell them not to leave their résumés in the copying machine when secretly job-hunting." "Nobody's that stupid," I laughed. "What do you mean? It happened to me," moaned the shamefaced Harvard lawyer.) Phone messages, invoices, and confidential memos should also be handled with discretion.

6. *Look rich.* Always appear well stocked with news (*especially* when hunting information.). The more that people think you know, the more they will tell you.

7. Remember, the company is family, so *don't go in for the quick killing.* Avoid gossip games that leave others feeling cheated. For example, skip the famous "Oh, by the way, one last thing" trick, where you slip in the *real* $64,000 question just as you're leaving. You can't get news from an office on the defensive.

8. *Guard against garble.* Office intelligence has got to be right—and clear! Pay attention to detail. (Who called whom *first* about what aspect of which account?) It may seem minutiae to you, but to those with the rest of the clues it may be the whole point of the story.

9. *Be generally upbeat.* Nonstop gloom is for the birds. Few rush to return the raven's call.

10. *Steer clear of the personal.* Let others report on romance.

11. Similarly, be above seeking and passing on the little scandals (who got refused a reserved parking space) to all but a handful of intimates. But *never be too good to listen.*

12. Relax with your "happy few"; be real, and dish some dirt. (Still, not the really awful dirt.) Even when indiscretion is best, one needn't overdo it.

## Three's Company

While you should have dozens of contacts, you should probably keep your "happy few" down to no more than three others. (Such cronies should be sufficiently up on your interests to listen and look out for you.) Find those whose work, style, smarts, and skill you respect, then start climbing with—not against—them! Best bets are go-getters from approximately your level whose different aptitudes and ambitions will complement, not compete, with yours until that final bottleneck at the top of the corporate pyramid.

Why three? Five easy reasons:

1. One is really too few to help. You'll need several pairs of watchful eyes and ears.
2. Pacts are harder to break when you've pledged allegiance to—and so potentially put yourself on the outs with—several others.
3. Similarly, solidarity is enforced by more watchdogs.
4. There's strength in numbers, especially when you want to push a particular story line.
5. Finally, fail-safe. You'll still be covered should some of your cronies fall by the wayside.

While no *entente cordial* may last forever, don't get this close to colleagues you don't anticipate liking for at least a decade.

## Office Romance

A few words to the wise:

1. The expressions are many ("Don't get laid where you get paid," "Don't shit where you eat"): inelegant, but eloquent. Bad news for both sexes, office romance is fatal for women. The word on the most innocuous affair can undo years' worth of Brooks Brothers blue-suited dress-for-successing. Suddenly you're no longer "Jane who closed the Krups deal" but "Jane, you know—the long, tall blonde, Tom Dowling's mistress."

2. I don't care if you both change taxis three times before meeting at the Ramada Inn in Trenton, New Jersey, if you're seeing someone at the office there is no way that everyone from the mail clerk to the president won't be talking about it. Who does what to and for whom? What do they see in each other? Aren't they getting married? Hasn't he started seeing someone else? Weren't they up to something under the table the other night? Who's on top? (Snicker, snicker.) God help you if you're into more modern living.

3. And if you break up? You'll have to deal with epithets like "Don Juan," "playmate," or "bitch" for the rest of your tenure. You two may handle it like adults—but that won't help you much if nobody else will.

4. Don't start an office romance unless you plan to marry your colleague and have checked out company rules on nepotism. While same-level management marriages sometimes make it, if one of you is "sleeping up" the corporate ladder, your colleagues will never stop talking. Win or lose, such mergers are legend!

## The Limits of Technique

"*Je ne suis point folle du technique, vous savez*" ("I'm not mad for technique"), remarked the call girl de luxe. And neither should you be. Fancy footwork that's fine on the outside backfires in the company's closed, court-like atmosphere. Joblobbying by planted rumor, for instance, rubs all but the weakest lions the wrong way and so works to your disadvantage.

## Inside Out

**Some of your best sources on the company don't even work there.** Most employees are aware of the company's hothouse atmosphere and are pretty well programmed not to tell *each other* company secrets. But as those who leave the firm soon discover, such taboos don't extend to office alumni. (Where else can the insider find an audience who knows the cast but won't be running into the characters on a daily basis?) Knowing this, you should keep up on present company by regularly debriefing former colleagues.

**Ex-colleagues aren't the only outsiders with the inside story.** The competition knows tons about you, too! Go to trade meetings and conventions. (So what if nothing of "substance" ever happens.) Dive in there and make contacts; then keep in guarded touch with select competitors.

**Another important outside source will probably be your industry's suppliers.** So keep it friendly. Your boss may try to cover up the fact that the magazine is folding, but the paper people will tell you he hasn't bought enough stock to print the next issue. While contacts within your company could fill you in, they pay a higher penalty for talking.

Similarly, while colleagues probably know much the same things as you, even underlings in companies working with yours may know more. (After all, their bosses are busy keeping their own company's secrets!)

## Professional Secrets

**On your case:** Who said lawyers don't tell? While lawyers (like doctors) are bound by oath not to betray the clients' confidences, God (and the American Bar Association) knows they do! But discreetly—or so they think. Perhaps they don't mention the client's name, but they go on in such lawyerly detail that if you've any sense of their field and client list you can fill in the names yourself. And once the case is over, they're home free. (It's "legal history" then, not gossip.) Especially if another lawyer asks; talk is always free round "the bar." Just pray they don't start teaching your case (complete with telling anecdotes) in next year's torts course.

### Tight-lipped Money Men—*Don't Bank on It!*

And if you thought lawyers were bad . . . Like the sexy spy, the tight-lipped banker is less fact than fiction. After all, a banker is but a glorified salesman, with an interest in letting you know his services are in demand just like any other salesman. When two bankers are playing squash and one says, "Well, Chase really beat you out on the Rat Racers Auto deal," the other is bound to come back with, "Rat Racers? Hah! They actually came to me first. They may have a reputation for cunning in the marketplace—but I wouldn't lend them a nickel! Their whole financial structure's rotten!" Something about a pinstriped suit lends such authority to sour grapes! While prudence dictates great discretion about the finances of current customers, when a firm switches banks . . . should old business acquaintances be forgot? Common practice says no. Once an account, always a story.

### Who Watches the Watchers?

You should! While you needn't go so far as to date Justice Department and SEC employees, many have done so (with excellent results). At the very least, be a discreet friend to industry analysts and reporters; they know volumes. Just don't *you* say much, unless you're planting something. Whatever your lion may say, no one really likes to see his assistant quoted in the *Wall Street Journal*.

**Musts:** *The Fine Art of Finding Out*

The following are musts for surveying the company:

1. *Positioning is paramount.* Once you get a job that puts you "in the loop," whatever you don't come across you can easily trade for.
2. *Plan ahead.* Top brass is always searching for good staffers. Be self-sacrificing. Break raw youths in and pass them on. It's the next best thing to your being there.
3. For general flotsam and jetsam, touch base with a liaison twice a week.
4. When you're after something specific for a legitimate reason (you're thinking of hiring someone, for instance), you can call up almost anyone and ask straight out; just tell them why you need to know and how you plan to use their information. (Will you pass it on? Might it become part of a written report? And, if so, seen by whom, under what constraints? Will you be sourcing?) Simply addressing your sources' worries will do much to relieve them. It's absolutely staggering how much even strangers will tell if given even half a reason.
5. *Teamwork.* If you've absolutely no excuse for asking, ask one of your cronies to ask for you. Amusingly enough, the fact that a colleague has requested they ask then becomes their own legitimate reason for asking. Don't hesitate to ask cronies to make such inquiries for you, and stand ready to reciprocate: it's yet another way to expand your network and get others in the "habit of telling." (While it's perfectly acceptable to ask an equal why he wants to know, to then question the reason, however ludicrous it may be, is *causus belli,* for bitter bureaucratic warfare.)

## Tricks of the Trade

All the business school texts warn never tell more than you hear. How staggeringly simplistic! Whenever you swap shop talk, the information traded is but one part of a complex transaction embracing power, access, friendship, and information accounts past, present, and future. (You may never tell me a single story, while I faithfully report everything, yet, if you promote my prospects with the boss, we both may be happy with the bargain.) This host of variables makes it near impossible to measure an even swap, let alone make one. (Is a story's value judged by the risks the teller runs? by its general newsworthiness? or by its specific career or entertainment value to the hearer?) When someone feels cheated on news, odds are the "shop-talk swindle" is only part of a whole relationship gone sour.

Each trade is unique, but you can't go wrong using these four rules as guide:

1. Don't count too closely. Few warm to an anal/compulsive trading partner.
2. Tear up the books with cronies. Just tell them what they need to know, whether or not they even know they need to ask you.
3. With noncronies: volunteer only the most innocuous news —unless you're offering it up as a special bond-building favor.
4. Start small. Don't *you* get into the habit of telling before they establish credit.

## The Joy of Counter-cyclical Inquiry

The joy of counter-cyclical inquiry is but a corollary of that larger, oft-neglected truth: every question is not worth asking. While some searches expand your network, others cost you. The same source who balks at slipping you word on the status of your vacation request, might have warned you of an upcoming reorganization, had you not pressed for the more trivial news earlier.

Similarly, don't trade for stories of the sort you don't want to be known for: petty, mean-spirited chatter on colleagues' misfortunes, sex lives, expense scandals, etc. Neither do you want to be seen as checking up on close chums (unless you indicate that you're checking up in order to "straighten out" a story). Nor should you be caught trading for information that someone in your position would have, if he enjoyed his boss's confidence. Also, don't waste time chasing after updates on the latest rumor not involving you directly. (It will all come out over drinks once the dust has settled.) In sum, don't bother chasing after news you can't affect, don't really need, and will soon be given anyway.

Why badger the office manager into slipping you advance word of the salary increases you'll all compare over lunch tomorrow? However, if a week earlier you had learned that your boss was wavering over what increase to give *you*, you might have weighed in with a timely memo updating developments on a recent highly profitable project you manage. The smart corporate gossip is far more interested in word on what's still being discussed than news of what has already been decided. Or conversely, get the full debriefing once the heat is off. Get the full story on why you didn't make partner last spring through inquiries made in July when such news is less tightly held. It will help you in the next round.

## Let It Be

Every now and then (when he's being secretly wooed by the competition, for instance) even your best friend might hold back. Let it be. Have you heard a chum is about to be fired or promoted, yet he says nothing? Don't push if it's not crucial to your own career. Odds are the issue hasn't been decided and he's afraid to tip the balance by talking about it.

# 10 · Speculation

> Shouldn't I be at liberty to assume that he doesn't know what he's saying, if he's insane enough to give me this information?
>
> WITTGENSTEIN, *On Certainty*

---

IF succeeding *inside* the corporate gossip game is like playing chess, *outside* one plays a wild, one-handed Space Invaders, with luck, speed, skill, native wit, wariness, and basic killer instincts all coming into play. Especially those killer instincts! While corporate intrigues resemble those of a royal court, the general market is more like California during the Gold Rush, with greedy swarms sifting the dirt, quizzing and misleading one another as each hustles that elusive make-a-million stake.

Generally, we like to know things first because it enhances our sense of self-importance. But in business we're after more than ego-gratification. We need to know what's happening first so that we can buy before the herd hears, rushes in, and drives up prices. Whatever our line, the basic trading strategy is to find an undervalued asset, buy it for a song, then turn around and sell it for what it's really worth—or better still, treble that! As more venture capitalists chase proportionately fewer diamonds in the rough, early access to accurate intelligence on winning deals grows ever more important.

While corporate injunctions against tricking colleagues spring largely from self-interest, this still enforces a certain code. Outside, depending on the size of your business circle, almost the only rule is that there are no rules. Whatever you can pull off is permitted.

"There's a saying in real estate. You shake hands on a deal and then you count your fingers," explains one entrepreneur who found action as a marine in 'Nam fine basic training for the rigors of the Manhattan real estate scramble. "I couldn't believe it at first. I was buying a couple of buildings from this guy who's practically my mentor—yet I look at the contract and it's not what we agreed to at all. He's trying to kill me! Our attorneys are still wrangling when he comes to me with a second deal. 'Look,' he says, 'you know I'm getting old and can't manage things the way I used to, so I want you to forget the first deal, and come in with me on something better.' He says he has heard some nearby waterfront is buyable, but of course he won't tell me who's talking 'cause he's afraid I might find the seller and make my own bid. Now, should I give up the first deal? Everything might be just as Harry says—or maybe there's no waterfront to be had at all. Maybe what he has *really* heard is something that makes that *first* property more valuable! Of course, I could ask around, but I don't want to alert other potential buyers! Should I trust Harry? 'Look, Tom,' says a friend, 'if you trusted Harry, he'd be disappointed in you.'"

The trouble is, you can't check out a hot tip. True or false, if it's really hot, no one else will have heard of it yet! Ask around and, instead of sleuthing out hard news, all you end up doing is alerting others to your "exclusive."

## To Bribe or Not to Bribe

Should you ever resort to bribery to get the inside scoop? A wide range of business types consulted advised against it. (I know, what were they *supposed* to say? But at least *some* of them were being honest.) The arguments against offering cold cash for hot tips are three: scruples, scandal (should you get caught), and, finally, a sense that there should be *some* limits.

"I'd see it as an admission I can't do my job," explained one East Coast film executive. That said, no one interviewed really considered anything short of cold cash as a bribe: "Of course, I want good things to happen to people who help me," our film exec explains. "That's part of what we're trading."

"Bribing people for inside stuff is like industrial spying," says a former government official turned aerospace exec. "There's so much back and forth, engineers working first for this company, then for the competitor, that the bribe is rarely so gross as an envelope full of cash. But it's understood that part of what a guy's selling when he trades up to his next job is his ability to stay tuned in to talk at his old office."

## Raiders

"You have to keep as low a profile as possible. The trick is to get the deal as close to wrapped up as you can before exposing your hand, even to your bankers," one corporate raider whispers over Perrier at a corner table of his club. Once partner in a large investment banking firm, my source left to start his own firm for finding, buying, and reorganizing undervalued companies. Whether flying, phoning, or entertaining, his life is one long quest for news on "the company that can be bought." His objective: find it before bigger buyers drive the price up; *then* turn the company around and sell it to them. It's a complex, fast-moving, big-stakes game played with monies from around the world for assets all around the country. As with real estate, the trick is picking up the tips, evaluating them, and raising large amounts of money without letting anyone else learn enough to "steal the deal." Give-a-little, get-a-little only goes for gossip about *others'* pursuits. The smart raider wraps up his own deals before others can even guess where he's looking. This is no easy task when each day thousands of financial analysts are also searching for that winning "find." Your best shot at hot tips is through networking. Better still, back-channel networking.

"I worked hard building contacts with local bankers, lawyers, and business people. Now I have a nationwide grapevine totally independent of major financial centers. Still, once you hear of a deal you have to bring an expert in to evaluate it, and this can lead to leaks," our raider explains, grimacing.

"You have to give to get, but sometimes you get burned," sighs another venture capitalist. "Once my partner tried to hire the president of the firm we were buying's competition. We let this guy look at the books; next thing we knew his old company buys the thing right out from under us!"

When millions hang in the balance, a handshake sometimes doesn't count for much. "I learned a real expensive lesson on that one. Now I'm tighter with my clearances than the Pentagon." What about "shop talk" as dinner party chatter? "Oh, it's important to shoot the breeze, but if I talk about it socially it's never something I'm really after."

"Information is everything. All sorts of speculations are factored into investment decisions. Whether this stock is a good buy now depends on what happens to interest rates, to Poland, to the money supply, to Reagan, management's mood; nobody knows, but everybody guesses," shrugs one top financial analyst.

## Put Your Money Where Your Mouth Is

"Still, street gossip is pretty reliable," another capitalist ventures over lunch at the club. "Even the more personal stuff—because we pick up on people's lives *as* they relate to business interests. Word that the head of a major conglomerate was mad for a girl half his age wouldn't sweep the street—unless she was an actress and he was buying her a studio. It isn't news that someone is telling friends he's thinking of taking it easier—unless the guy is head of City Investing. Then that rumor means he's ripe to sell. In which case I'm not just interested, I'm on the phone putting together an offer! But strictly personal news—I haven't the time.

Given the choice, I want to know what company, and not which girl, the competition's courting."

"Smart people may sometimes intentionally mislead you," says Street Smarts, "but deal news doesn't get that garbled in transmission. Sure, when a company like Conoco is up for grabs, you may hear that everyone from Mobil to the Pope is about to bid. But while in the end Dupont may walk off with the prize, that doesn't necessarily mean the earlier talk was wrong. When the smoke clears you often find the Vatican actually did set up a line of credit!"

## Impressarios of Gossip

Corporate takeovers are a gossip maven's delight. The Plugged-in Peter who "guesses" which small company is going to be gobbled up (and have its stock bid up by hungry giants) stands to make a killing. Takeover attempts can last days, weeks, or stretch on into months of complications during which time the Street is abuzz with tips betted by the high-rolling men in the risk arbitrage department.

An investment banking firm's risk arbitrageurs work behind locked doors in what are called "clean rooms." "They're playing with the firm's money and they don't want the other partners breathing down their backs," Street Smart explains. But the risk arbitrageurs' isolation from anyone with news is totally imaginary. Much like the ace reporter, they spend every waking minute hustling word of what key players are up to. "It's people knowing people," one Wall Street insider explains. "Those guys are regular impresarios of gossip!" "They've got more 'best friends' than most ordinary people have nodding acquaintances!" laughs another investment banker. Why would a Justice Department official pass one risker valuable word that talk was the SEC would block a bid? The same reason why an officer of a target company might tip a trader to his board's leanings. Payola? "Naw," says Street Smart. "People are just people. Telling inside stories makes them feel important."

## Tipping: *The Secret Scandal of Inside Trading*

> *Truscott:* Now then, sir, be reasonable. What has just happened is perfectly scandalous and better go no farther than these three walls. It's not expedient for the general public to have its confidence undermined. You'd be doing the community a grave disservice by revealing the full and frightening facts of this case.
>
> JOE ORTON, *Loot*

Sometimes trading inside talk is a deal in itself: even before a bid is announced I tell you what's coming up in return for a similar scoop or a share of your profits from my tip. Such "inside trading" is illegal because officers cash in at ordinary stockholders' expense. It is also widespread. One reliable source who monitored corporate takeovers for a major New York bank said that when he was stockwatching only about thirty percent of the takeovers didn't show an inside profit-taking pattern. Incredible? "No, that's about right," said a corporate lawyer also present.

**Don't wash dirty linen in the Street: talk of this scandal goes no further than the family.** Wall Street types like to pretend that the few inside traders caught and prosecuted each year are the only culprits, but for each inside-trader caught, a thousand become millionaires! "You can do it with names behind names behind names. The money moves from New York to Canada, then maybe back through New York to London before passing through Switzerland on its way back to New York, where you go short on the acquiring company and long on the stock of the company being acquired. Really, it's not hard," one young English banker assures me, deftly rolling a joint. "Inside trading is like speeding: there's nothing wrong with it except that it's illegal."

## You've Got to Have Friends

"Don't you see? Information is currency. It's crazy to regulate it. Look at the gossip in a market like Hong Kong," sighs a banker. "No regulations there! Everyone worth anything is wired into everything. The clan thing may be feudal, but it gives you the most sophisticated financial news network around. You can't *touch* the Chinese when it comes to gossip!"

While all the gossip passed between old school chums is not so hot it's illegal, it's no accident that the most recent inside trading scandals involve classmates from exclusive, ultra-competitive "B" schools like Harvard. Indeed, one pretty Harvard grad, recently front-page in another corporate scandal, is also rumored to have been the first to offer illegal inside tips as alimony! Her abandoned husband cashed in. She got out. They got away with it. Does one laugh? weep? or chalk one up to liberation?

## Honor Among Thieves: *Why Open Secrets Are Kept Quiet*

> There are no secrets better kept than those which everybody guesses.
>
> G. B. SHAW, *Mrs. Warren's Profession*

"People are extremely jealous of their reputations," one Raider notes. "They're either known as backroom fixer types or straight shooters." But losing is losing, and winning is everything. As with lawyers, agents, and other hired guns, certain kinds of scandalous behavior are viewed less as blemishes than as beauty marks. "So long as they're on 'our side,' better shrewd if shady than honest to a fault." "Despite a flattering supposition to the contrary, people come readily to terms with power," Galbraith notes. Open secrets stay secret because it's professional suicide for anyone to stand up and say, "I know it for a fact," after the powers that be have pronounced the story "just a rumor."

**But lest you get too disillusioned ...** A few people *are* still scrupulously honest about their use of hot gossip. "I have access to a lot of information I could legally use and profit from, but doing so would make me feel uncomfortable. There are, you know, a lot of Conocos around," crack investment adviser Alan Greenspan smilingly told the *Times*. And one smiles to hear him. Of course, Greenspan never went to Harvard . . .

## Money Talks

> In foreign currency markets widely held expectations tend to be quickly self-fulfilling.
> ROBERT SOLOMON, "The U.S. and the World Economy,"
> *Foreign Affairs*, 1981

But let's leave Wall Street's investment types behind for the moment and talk pure money, as traded in international currency markets.

"The dollar opened lower against the mark because of rumors that the Bundesbank would increase its interest rates on loans to commercial banks from the current 7.5 percent. But the dollar strengthened later in the day when the bank announced it was going to leave the rate unchanged. . . ."

"The pound sank to $1.9385 at the close of European trading today, continuing its dramatic plunge against the American currency amid expectations of a cut in the price of North Sea oil and a belief that the current high level of U.S. interest rates would be maintained. . . ."

"A cut in the price of Mexican oil as well as rumors of a cut in the price of North African oil have led to speculation that the British National. . . ."

Any chance clipping of currency notes would show the same startling (to the layman) recurrence of the words "rumor," "expectations," and "speculation." Indeed, these three weird sisters are the bids by which the world's largest floating crap game (international currency trading) is played.

"A banker friend was in Argentina when a government official told him the Argentinian peso would be devalued in two weeks, and sure enough, it was," recalls one multinational's money trader. "If we hadn't heard and hedged, we could have been killed. These devaluations can cut currency value by thirty percent: more than we make there in a whole year dodging bullets!"

A good currency trader keeps up on a world of developments. How does he do it? By keeping constantly on the phone, hooked up to his Reuter's screen, and by making frequent globe-trotting tours to strengthen ties with his best sources, the international bankers. "We talk to these guys several times each day—the Swiss, Morgan in Frankfurt, Chase in London." While multinationals account for fifteen percent of the currency traded, the prime money movers are the banks. Not that the banks are always in the know. Foreign exchange losses are what led to the collapse of Franklin National. "Sure, the authorities get nervous when they think the banks are just gambling the market. But they're always in there for themselves, not just for clients!"

"The European markets open between three and four A.M. New York time. So you're already in the office catching up on overnight news by six A.M. or seven," explains one crack currency trader. When the sun (and market) move on, our friend doesn't just fold up his tent and go home. "Tokyo doesn't open until eight P.M. our time, and nothing happens in Hong Kong until eight-thirty."

"When you first roll in, you just generally shoot the breeze. Things like 'Has the Bundesbank been in the market?' 'Have the Italian postal workers settled yet?' The usual stuff. One of the best tricks for picking up news is to get a real neophyte and pick his brains, or go to lunch with someone who loves to brag." Another favorite ploy? Talking to Japanese traders here in New York. "They have to file regular detailed reports with Tokyo, so they've always just talked with a lot of people and are good for the latest." Speaking of reports, what about reporters? "You know, it's really a shame," Top Trader sighs. "You'd think they'd be great sources, but they just don't understand the subject." Top's comment was echoed by a number of other traders. (Perhaps in part because they feel a bit competitive.) For a trader, too, is "only as good as his instincts and his sources." With even a half-point shift meaning millions on big positions, traders are poised to act on the first hint of rumors about upcoming rumors. "It's really sort of a never-never land. When I hear something, my first concern isn't whether it's actually true, but whether other traders hearing it are going to buy it and trade on that basis—*or* whether *they* may not believe it but guess others will and so buy it themselves anyway," explains a trader. "Our games can make the spy-versus-counterspy stuff look straightforward!"

"It's really psychological warfare," agrees a Morgan trader turned consultant. "A trader doesn't just trade, he spends most of his day bouncing ideas [some might say rumors] around the world. Will people buy and sell on my say-so? That depends on whether they think I'm 'talking my book,' that is, trying to talk up a currency I've got so I can unload it for a profit." With money talk, as with other rumors, the less seemingly self-interested your motive, your credibility increases.

"Say I call up a trading friend in Frankfurt and say, 'What have you heard about Soviet mobilization on the Polish border?' No big deal, I just sort of drop it in. I guarantee you, within two minutes every major trader in the world would be chewing on that one. Why don't I just say it flat out? Two things. If I preface my rumor with 'Do you think this can be true?' no one can ever come back and accuse me of lying. But even more important, rumor flies faster when phrased as a question. If I act like I'm in the dark too, the other guy is less on the defensive. He may even call back a few hours later to say, 'Look, I called a friend in Zurich who called a friend of the Quai d'Orsay who said the rumors about Soviet mobilization are totally unfounded.' But by then I've already cashed in on the rumor, sparked by my question."

## Look Who's Talking

How does the sharp dealer evaluate the dozens of rumors he hears each day? Each trader gets a worldwide reputation for good information, skittishness, or caution. *Motive* is the real bitch. "Each time I hear something," sighs Smart Money, "I have to stop and wonder, Is he telling me this because he's long on, say, dollars, or is he actually short but thinks that if he talks them up, I'll *think* he's long and start unloading mine, which he can then pick up at a bargain?"

Don't good ties keep some traders from BSing each other? "Generally, the farther down the success ladder you become friends, the more you trust each other later," says one trader who turns to fellow preppies in a crunch. "Still . . . if I'm in the middle of something big, I just can't tell even close friends until afterwards. Why send them into the market to bid against me?"

## Informed Sources

"Sometimes if you're in early on a hot rumor, you call the Federal Reserve and check; they usually say they'll call you back and often do," explains one trader. "It's not that they want to help me out so much as put a lid on the market before it goes crazy." But even official sources aren't above sparking false rumors in the national interest. Talking with a top European banker just before the Ottawa Summit, Fed chairman Volker implied that interest rates would soon be slashed (which would make the dollar drop). The banker was no sooner off the line than he told his traders to sell dollars. Which they did, passing word on to their friends just as soon as they'd finished their own transaction. Soon everybody heard Volker's 'tip,' dumped dollars, and down the dollar plunged, heading off allies' complaints about "dear" dollars planned for the Ottawa Summit. The only catch: after the summit, U.S. interest rates kept climbing.

"Let's face it, we were suckered by Volker." Smart Money shrugs. Can't traders who got burned complain? "What are you going to do? Stop talking to the Fed?" asks a trader. "Besides, whenever smart officials give tips they phrase it so that *they're* not outright saying it, *you're reading it."* The Fed's role in the currency gossip game is called "talking up" or "talking down" the dollar.

## Taking Stock

The Security and Exchange Act of 1933 makes deliberate use of rumor to manipulate stock prices illegal. But again, one need only glance at business page headlines ("Polaroid's Stock Rises on Rumors," "Hutton Up 5 on Merger Rumors") to see that the SEC's antirumor rule hasn't stopped talk. There's just no escaping it: rumor rules uncertain situations, and the market is just such a situation.

"The Wall Street information hierarchy goes something like this," Street Smart explains. "Truly inside are the investment bankers and large capital managers. Then you have your institutional analysts and institutional brokers, with the commercial bankers like your major corporate treasurers sort of off to one side, sometimes in, sometimes out. Way at the bottom you have retail stock brokers, guys who only hear after everyone else has, yet who pawn it all off as the latest to some rich matron from Philadelphia. The news may be stale stuff indeed, but the come-on is always the same. 'Buy this stock. I've got a hot tip on a winner.' Whenever you hear about a 'hot' tip at a party, turn and run the other way! If there's *one* thing you can still bank on, it's that people who go around giving out 'hot' tips for free just don't know what they're talking about!"

One nonfinancial friend tells of passing on word that a company we'll call American Drug was about to get FDA approval for a herpes cure. At least he *thought* he said American Drug. Later in the week when he told the tale again at another soirée, the man standing next to him gasped, "But I thought you said *U.S. Drug!*" and rushed off to call his broker.

"Rich people are crazy!" roared my friend. "Can you imagine actually putting money on a stock tip someone like *me* dropped at a screening?" The trouble is people assume that experts in one field give good advice in others. Far from it. Judge a man's news by his credentials on the topic at hand. Don't take stock tips from a porn tycoon or buy real estate on the advice of a hot literary agent.

## Self-fulfilling Prophecies

The phrase *self-fulfilling prophecy* rolls trippingly from the tongue—so trippingly, in fact, that we tend to overuse it. When the smart tipster talks, the vulgarians follow—up to a point. (Even lemmings swarm into the sea only occasionally.) Take the case of stock-casting showman Joseph Granville. When Granville wired his well-heeled clients to "sell everything," they not only sold, they told others who sold and told, and so on, sending the Dow down nearly 24 points on January 7, 1981, with Mr. Granville's say-so generally held to be the precipitating factor. In September Granville decided doomsday would strike again—on Monday, September 28, to be exact ("Blue Monday," as Granville dubbed it in advance). But this time, instead of simply wiring his many clients and having them pass it on, adding the cumulative weight of *their* belief to his word (and keeping the all-important "word of mouth" inside-tip aura), Granville blew it by making his announcement on that least exclusive of all media, television. After a few bad hours on "Blue Monday" morning, Wall Street rallied in defiance. After all, whoever heard of getting a hot tip from the *Today Show?* Really, Mr. Granville! It's a blue Monday indeed when an Oz like you forgets that *the hottest talk starts with a whisper, not an announcement.*

# PART FOUR

# ADVANCED

# The Circle Game– Social Work

# 11·Haute Biche Is Back!

> Love and scandal are the best sweeteners of tea.
> HENRY FIELDING *Love in Several Masques*

"SOCIETY? I just visit my friends," the late society queen Babe Paley used to say. A bit of a fib, yet the perfect response, all the same.

This section is subtitled "Social Work" because many still devote much time, toil, money, sweat, and tears to winning social standing—and making it look easy! (In even the hardest of hearts, it seems, the craving for acceptance beats second only to the will to power.) Social climbing is also a most practical sport. Whether you want to legitimize your fortune or simply increase it, having the right friends never hurts. But while *having* the right friends never hurts, *acquiring* them often does. As every arriviste knows, forcing oneself upon Society is never easy. (Indeed, if it were, why bother?) Yet while one must assiduously plan one's entry and plot one's rise, one must never admit to harboring social ambitions—or even admit that social distinctions exist. (Except, of course, when *tête-à-tête* with other People Like Us.) Good breeding, Mark Twain explains, consists in hiding how much we think of ourselves and how little we think of the other fellow.

Actually it's not quite that simple. Since here in the States "old money" can refer to any family loot more than a decade old,

"Society" is understandably fluid—and chaotic. Yes, social consciousness is out, opulance and elitism back in—but with a difference. Instead of the old "whole hog" conspicuous consumption of the fifties and early sixties, we now favor a certain guarded excess best characterized by an important arbiter who pronounced a recent Paris collection "the kind of clothes you could wear to watch a revolution and not get shot in."

As it is with fashion, so it goes with modern life-styles. One no longer aspires to be avant-garde, but center right. "I tell you, I'm worried," one silver-haired jet-setter confides over espresso. "With twelve-year-olds snorting coke and plumbers at orgies, the only thing left for a truly decadent person is to be square." Pity the poor aristocrat picking his way through the swarming vulgarians! Lacking the neat rules of the English class system, with our own sketchy mores nearly shredded by the sixties' social revolutions, American society doesn't quite know how to sort itself out. (Not surprising when you consider its roots: part meritocracy, part plutocracy, and part Jeffersonian Democracy to equal parts maître d's whim, publicist's will, and editor's way.)

But society must have rules. Lacking such rules we become ever more obsessed with finding them, and this debate on what's in, what's out, what's "shameless," "clever," and "acceptable" behavior is the very heart of social gossip.

Think back a moment to the last few stories you may have heard. The moral is often only too explicit. ("Bad enough that she should marry him, but then to leave after six months!" "It's one thing to be greedy, but quite another to expect us all to act as if his latest trash is *art!*") Gossip's meaning rests in the way the anecdote is framed and in the spin given the story. Sometimes the exception proves the rules. ("Who" overshadows "what.") A passing reference to scandal may be a sort of praise, its subtext being: "Tom has such style he can pull off even the most flagrant indiscretions." After a ritual "You won't believe what Tom did," such "slander" ends on an admiring "only Tom . . .": your cue that while Tom's caper gets high marks, you'd better not try it.

## Pecking Order: *You Can't Tell the Players Without Knowing the Gossip*

> *Paris*— "Who are all these people?" Diana Ross whispered to Patrice Calmettes, her companion the other night at Andre Oliver's. "High Society," he replied, and Ross looked suitably impressed. "So that's who they all are," she smiled.
>
> *W*, December 11, 1981

*"Ma passion la plus vive et la plus chère est celle de ma dignité et de mon rang"* ("Status has been my grand passion"), confesses the duc de Saint-Simon, whose marvelously bitchy memoirs of life at Versailles establish him as one of history's premier gossips. As it was then, so it still is today: Society is a game about rank, with gossip serving both as simultaneous scoreboard and play-by-play interpretation.

But how to get "too in for out"?—that's the puzzle! Consider for the moment the myriad questions posed by just the humble preposition *in*. Get "in" where? And, once "there," which people, tables, and types are "in" enough to chat up? Which styles are suitable for sporting? Which drugs are cool enough to snort, shoot, smoke, or gargle? Which ideas are hot enough to spout? Even the straight mind boggles. Small wonder then that this year alone more words were wasted on worrying, "what's in?" than have been spilt over the whole interminable course of arms control negotiations. While the latter are esteemed as "diplomacy," serious sorts deride the former as "just gossip."

Such serious souls protest too much. Much of the time they're supposedly arguing issues, they're also talking "ins" and "outs." ("Is Cap back in with the White House?" "Will Regan leave Treasury?") But imagine, if you will, a scene where the race for place is played without benefit of covering commitment to policy or profit. Flash back to the biting in/out anxiety of adolescence; add the con man, courtesan, or bishop's devotion to proper form and nuanced feel for the magic of the right robes, rich sets, and ritual incantation ("Henry," "Jackie," "Gstaad"); throw in a twist of cynicism, a liberal dash of envy, *et voila:* Society. Welcome to Paris, Manhattan, Palm Beach, or any watering hole the world over. Dance right up and meet Philip ("just a gigolo") Junot, or sidle up to Nancy Reagan's favorite Mouth about Town, First Escort Jerry Zipkin, for the lowdown on what little dinner is not to be missed and which overeager couple gave a sit-down dinner for thirty-six when, *dahhrling,* everyone *knows* twelve to twenty-four is this season's cozy number. Or check out that indefatigable globe-trotting socialite, "Knock-about Nan" Kempner, a toothy stick of a woman so very avant-garde she devoted her life to shopping, years before the "me decade" had even started! Then there's that *absolutely charming* couple so admired for the perfect elegance of their oh-if-you-could-only-be-there-too entertainments that the usually stolid *New York Times Sunday Magazine* couldn't resist featuring the glittering pair of barracudas on their cover! (She's known in her own right for a little black book the size of the O.E.D. and for switching place cards at other people's dinners.)

"It's hard to believe," moaned one long-time "social worker" clutching her pearls. "Before the War no serious socialite would have dreamed of courting Seventh Avenue."

But with the postwar flux came chaos. If almost anyone could be in, how could the discriminating discriminate? One could turn to talk, of course, asking one's friends. But why take their word for it? (They were, after all, *your* friends!) Among arrivistes, it's always the Age of Anxiety.

"There was always some glamour attached to good-looking foreigners," says one who knew Jackie when she was but a Bouvier cruising her first millionaire. "Cassini used to write about his brother Oleg. But it was John Fairchild who really shook things up. His *Women's Wear Daily* made showing off acceptable— even *desirable."* Gone was the old Society dictum that a lady's name should appear in the paper but three times (born, married, died). Gone too was the divine self-assurance of Fitzgerald's golden, sociopathically careless Tom and Daisy. In was the Brash New World where even the Bluest Bloods smiled for the camera and made nice with Society reporters. Designing rag traders supped with Vanderbilts, who now designed jeans. "All John Fairchild's fault," the social veteran mutters.

**Arriving in Style:** *Get out Your Women's Wear!*

While the elegantly peripatetic scion of the Fairchild Publications family has undeniably brought rags to riches, millenium-old sumptuary laws show that who wears what has long been a hot topic. If the clothes don't quite make the man, they do make a clear statement of his pretensions. As the easiest "class" attribute to acquire, dress is also the first to be slashed to ribbons by sharp-tongued betters. Thus, Napoleon's foreign minister Talleyrand (whose own patent dated from Charlemagne) dished *"les merveilleuses,* the wives of nouveaux riches who took the place of the vanished ladies of the court, and who, like the latter, were imitated by sluts competing for the prize in luxury and extravagance." That is to say, even the gambling, thieving, womanizing, excommunicated ex-bishop still felt that something was "sacred": the privilege of one of "class" like himself to dish tarty *nouvelles* like the upstart empress!

Today, clothes are still central to class word wars. Just as *Rolling Stone* rose out of rock, so *W* sprang forth to guide the Drooling Class, an elite distinguished not by its capacity to govern (grey technocrats take care of that), nor even to consume (who can't?), but by the sheer aching excess of their need. (Isn't mad pursuit of any desire the real Fountain of Youth, and Ponce de Leon's quest itself the elixir?)

Desire for what? Ah, there's the rub. With modern status symbols switching almost as fast as you can say "mass communications," the Drooling Class's first hunger was for an artist to give shape to their vague yearnings. Enter *W*, Professor of Desire, setting standards, awarding stars to good children ("★★★★ CeCe Kielselstein-Cord in Galanos," "★★★ Evangeline Bruce in Balenciaga, with Bill Paley") and sniping at the bad ("those very expensive clothes hangers Nan Kempner and Lynn Wyatt in identical Givenchy"). Tsk, tsk. Hate it? They *love* it. Punish me with hisses! Like many another thrill, the *joie d'arriver* draws much of its spice from our sense of sin. While the Noble Few sit safe above the fray, the parvenu stands exposed to shifting tastes and must take the cuts called. "Too in for out" today, "last year's fun couple" tomorrow. Such is the slippery life of style. "Entrances are made by fools like me, but only God can make a family tree."

## Blood Will Tell: *A Touch of Class*

> In Austria, "Man" begins at baron.
> PRINCE METTERNICH

"What a great advantage to be of noble birth, since it gives a man of eighteen the standing, recognition and respect that another man might not earn before he was fifty—that means winning thirty years start with no effort," a wistful Pascal notes. However glittering the aspirants, however often they ask their eternal "How'm I doing?" and the mirror—whether *People*, employees, or friends—answers, "You are the fairest of them all," there remains that nagging doubt. Our trousseau, table, and annual report may be impeccable, and yet . . . what, *au fond*, is our obsession with appearances, if not an attempt to finesse that deeper and more troubling mystery: class.

Who has and who hasn't really got class, that hottest of all social topics, with speculation on who has just how much class rivaled only by the gamesman's gossip about clout. But while clout affects only our projects, class cuts deep to what we feel about ourselves. Those aiming at clout no sooner achieve it than they seek to endow their clout with class. Given a strong will, strong purse, and above all, a strong stomach, social wonders may be wrought. Yet true class remains as elusive as divine election.

## What's in a Name? *The Word from the American "Aristocracy"*

> We've all been here for generations and all our cousins have married each other. I know people say that leads to insanity, but the real problem is everyone knows everybody's business before it happens.
>
> KITTY CLAIBORNE, a socialite in Richmond, Virginia, in *W*

"What's in a name? That which we call a rose by any other name would smell as sweet," observes the fatally naive Juliet. Smell as sweet, perhaps, but never fetch fifty dollars a dozen! Just so, aristocratic names impress even today. But is the aristocrat's gossip really all that different?

This urgent question buzzing in my brain, I scoured the archives and petitioned audiences with my betters. One such interview with a well-born liberal crusader so shocked my (admittedly unfashionable) democratic instincts that for a moment I feared I had strayed into Devrett's Registry. But no. Scratch a well-born liberal and find a Royalist.

"There's a kind of Milton Friedman principle at work in society," our Golden Boy explains with a winning grin. "Even at tremendous expenditure of time, money, and energy, a nouveau riche like Alan just can't buy himself in. No amount of Portuguese couples [as servants] can make you a part of Society." Well, well, take *that!* all you would-be Astors. Dress yourself up and trot about as you will, Society still knows its own. Most thoroughly. (Indeed, according to anthropologists, one only truly "belongs" when one is so up on the group's dirt that one can't unwittingly insult another member.) Our gossip bespeaks our "cultural competence."

Not that even bluebloods can't commit remarkable *faux pas*. Some, for instance, make the mistake of inviting famous artists, pols, and other creatures of the hour. "It's very gauche to be impressed with achievement," explains one blueblood.

This touchiness about the claims of mere ability cut to the skittish reactionary heart of all aristocratic dishing. Instead of savaging "eccentric" (read certifiable) Aunt Hélène or "jolly" (read drunken) Uncle George, the well-bred save their fire for the real threat: promising outsiders. One season a bright young playwright was invited to and dazzled all the salons in Paris. It was too much for his betters. "He hasn't even a name!" sniped one chevalier, taking the classic noble's line of attack. "True, but at least I'm making my name, while you're finishing yours!" Voltaire retorted, overhearing.

Clever Voltaire? Hardly. His comeback earned him a drubbing, the Bastille, and a brief exile to England. (The more absurd a claim, the more ferocious its adherents.) Of course, the happy philosopher would laugh last and best. But while the Revolution inspired by his Enlightenment would cost nobles their titles, lands, and heads—aristocratic airs die hard.

### Haute Biche Is Back!

*La charité n'impose pas l'obligation de ne pas voir les choses et les gens tels qu'ils sont.* (Kindness doesn't require we tell it like it isn't.)

SAINT-SIMON, *Mémoires*

Clearly "class" is not just a question of *who* you are, but of *what* you say and *how* you say it. Long a favorite of top talking heads, the Reagan Reaction has brought the aristocratic haute biche style back with a vengeance.

What is haute biche–style gossip? Deflationary darts. Elegantly incisive invective. A few examples will help explain (to keep it safe, I'll draw my illustrations from past classics). Our friend Saint-Simon's remark, *"Mme de Maintenon, par raison de ressemblance, aimait bien mieux les repenties que celles qui n'avait pas fait de quoi se repentir"* ("No angel herself, Mme. de Maintenon prefers repentant sinners to those lacking sins to repent"), was a nice haute biche slap at the courtesan's new-found virtue. The remark of Louis XIV's mistress Diane de Poitier, that "the years that a woman subtracts from her age are not lost; they are added to another woman's" is also haute biche. As is Talleyrand's remark of a noblewoman that "in order to avoid the scandal of flirting, she consents immediately."

As with all good gossip the two main ingredients of haute biche are intelligence and irony. Like the epigram (a form to which it's closely allied), the haute biche bit is basically a two-part movement. First, it sets forth and seems to accept at face value the pretensions of the party being dished (i.e., "she's not the type to flirt") only to turn a quick arabesque en l'aire, immediately shredding the hypocritical facade with a kicker ("because she consents immediately"). Like all "good" social gossip the haute biche bit need be neither terribly fair nor scrupulously accurate. Delivered with appropriately tony accent, its *intime, entre-nous* tenor invites complicity. This, coupled with its aristocratically disinterested brutality, telegraphic timing, and aphoristic quality of admitting no response, has, through the years, created a style even the guillotine couldn't silence.

Speaking of which, the discerning reader will no doubt have noticed that most of our examples are from the French. *Eh bien!* Only the French (and some of our own not-so-innocents abroad) join a sharp eye for social detail with a sly delight in pricking imposture. The Germans, by contrast, lack the right light touch. While your upper-crust Englishman's accent is always a pleasure, his snideness often suffers from a puerile, public school quality. And should one actually listen to *what* the Englishman is saying, one often finds him rambling on about a not quite exportable story. Still, when they're good, they're killing. In print, at least, nobody does it better than the British.

**Good style/bad faith: who gets hurt?** Some haute biches like to think their sniping radically subversive. But while haute biche always bites, it never goes for the jugular. It's more of a "love nip," a teasing way of marking other members of the group, and therefore essentially *conservative* in function. One may impale the few without embracing the many. (After all, "don't be dreary" is hardly a revolutionary maxim.) Indeed, those most often hurt by haute biche are not the objects of attack, but the careless speaker who plies this gay party mode in an inappropriate environment.

# 12 · The Hostess Gets the Mostest

> Without cruelty, no feast.
> NIETZSCHE, *Thus Spake Zarathustra*

WHY has the hostess, whose only apparent sin is offering us free meals, come in for generations of abuse? One might imagine it some lingering fallout from the fuzzy-minded sixties, did the evidence not point farther back. Obviously, she's a natural target for her entertaining sisters. But it's not just competitive bitchiness. Our sense of the hostess's "bad faith" is as old as the Romantic cult of Sincerity itself. Pity the poor hostess! While most get to do their backstabbing out back, the poor hostess betrays in the floodlit front parlor. Indeed, if nursemaids' stories can be believed, many of our finest hostesses were deftly dropping "B" list toddlers before other infants even knew their alphabet!

But the dear reader mustn't think I'm downing the brave ladies who brighten our dull little lives and deadly marriages—far from it! The good party satisfies our craving for community even as it fulfills our even more primal urge to run with the hunting pack. "How's Tom?" "Heard from Dick?" "What's Harry up to?" Twenty questions isn't just played at class reunions; party talk allows catch-up queries viewed with suspicion in less "friendly" surroundings.

And it's not just the conversation; the whole social ritual is a gold mine of intelligence to be squirreled away for future reference. (Or better still, told at tomorrow night's dinner.) Just one glance around the room offers the instant unvarnished update on everyone's standing. Breezing in late to an election-night dinner, I asked the hostess (whose politics I *thought* I knew), "How are we doing?" Her answer, *"Who* are *'we'?"* told all. There's no better place to spot the pecking order than at a party.

## The Circle Game

> Let me smile with the wise and feed with the rich.
> DR. JOHNSON, Boswell's *Life of Johnson*

While all great gossips may not have the means to entertain in style, all great hostesses are great gossips. Both functions revolve around access. "I can get to anyone within a day," no small social shaker told me over drinks at the Four Seasons, "but Françoise can get to anyone the world over as we sit here."

A wise man knows everything, the saying goes, but the shrewd man knows everyone. The good hostess does the shrewd man one better: knowing everything *about* everyone. "She knows who's available, who's looking to invest, and who's secretly ready to sell," a businessman notes. "I almost always call her first," says one political reporter of a Washington hostess. Whereas the gossip simply keeps in touch, the hostess brings those with news together under the most convivial circumstances. "One of the hostess's duties is to serve as procuress," noted the oh-so-social Proust.

"They're self-appointed cruise directors," snipes one socialite. "Born meddlers," snaps another. "They need to know what's happening so they can take credit for arranging it!" Which they often have done, insists one perennial extra man who swears that scarcely a week goes by without some hostess making inquiries about the "availability" of rich male friends. When such dinner dates "take," the hostess is understandably in seventh heaven, since each of the happy pair now owes her updates till still richer prospects due them part. As it is with crimes of the heart, so it goes with politics, art, and business. The power to invite gives the hostess great gossip-gathering opportunities, which, in turn, help her further fine-tune her guest list.

## The List and How to Make It

> Hostesses who entertain much must make up their parties as ministers make up their cabinets, on grounds other than personal liking.
>
> GEORGE ELIOT, *Daniel Deronda*

The guest list is the most gossip-worthy aspect of every party. First, gossip is used to get the "right" sorts there. The classic approach is to invite one "catch," dangling another "name's" acceptance as bait; then, after this first "name" has accepted, one goes after the original "name," using the other heavy's "will attend." Good general word of mouth on the hostess's circle also helps to attract the important; news of this, in turn, aiding her efforts to attract the even more important, and so on, step by slippery step up the social ladder. While some may dedicate their lives to revolution, rival hostesses engage in no less bitter social wars, each claiming that hers is the first circle. This *petit cercle d'invités* may itself be as vicious as a family around Christmas, yet such "friendly" internecine fire is nothing compared to the dirt each circle does the other. God knows, you'll get not one regret if you leak word you'll be turning even Somebodies away. The following Page Six note helped make an already hot ticket a scorcher:

> BIG scandal out in Hollywood. It seems that top literary agent Irving (Swifty) Lazar invited Truman Capote—and lots of other Beautiful People—to his annual watch-the-Oscars party at the Bistro Monday night. Truman wrote back saying, swell, and that his date that night would be Joanne Carson, Johnny's ex. Swifty wrote back saying, in effect, Truman, you're most welcome, but don't bring Joanne. Johnny and the current Mrs. C. will be coming and I don't want to upset them. And Swifty suggested, "You and Gore Vidal can hold

hands." Truman thought the entire affair hilarious but then Jody Jacobs, society columnist for the *L.A. Times*, got hold of Swifty's letter and printed it. Yesterday a note from Swifty arrived at Jody's house: "I would suggest," Swifty wrote, "that you watch the Oscars elsewhere."

*New York Post*, page 6

People, quite simply, want to go to parties that are the talk of the town. And they talk about those parties that enhance their status by numbering them among the select. "How was the party?" and "Tell me, who was there?" spring almost simultaneously from our lips. Indeed, the mark of an absolute smash is a party whose guest list is not only leaked before, but is literally printed in the next day's paper. *WWD* listed all Alluring Sixty-five at Jackie O's dinner for Diana Vreeland, while *The Washington Post* printed the list for the historic White House dinner President Carter gave for China's visiting vice-premier, Deng Xiaoping. (With all three living presidents, and assorted past and present secretaries of state and defense crowding the floor, I felt gypped when I discovered my dinner partner was only GM's chairman!) For weeks before the fête, the question on all Washington's lips was "Would Teddy be snubbed?" When an eleventh-hour invitation for challenger Kennedy finally arrived, there were new hot questions: once at the dinner, would Teddy snub the president, or vice versa? Would Dr. Kissinger snub the current national security adviser Brezinski? Would former feeble secretary of state Rogers have to sit in the kitchen? Would clean-cut Vance snub Machiavellian Kissinger? Would Kissinger cut Nixon? Or, or . . . Well, I think you begin to get the picture. One could dine out on stories of that "night to remember" for half a season! Actually, the surprise gossip hit of the evening featured not these Washington Star Wars, but Hollywood's own Shirley MacLaine, who, while diplomats squirmed, insisted on thanking the vice-premier for the loving hospitality offered on her trip to China, apparently unaware that the general she so effusively thanked was currently trying her "wonderful Chinese friends," the Gang of Four, for treason!

Let the papers pick up on Nixon's return; Shirley's foot-in-mouth was the delicacy at every Georgetown dinner the next evening.

Shirley's *faux pas* points up a special party problem. Those at the top basically like to party only with others at the top. But when all guests are chiefs, there are no Indians to admire them. Now the clever hostess often finesses this problem by "mixing worlds," that is, one "A" couple from TV, another from the arts, a third from finance.

"I think people don't mind being invited just because they're important," one model hostess explains. "The trouble is, though, sometimes 'who's who' in the arts may know next to nothing about 'who's who' in Wall Street—and care less. Now *that* is the disaster party, one where your guests have absolutely no gossip in common."

Another entertainer believes you can mix worlds, up to a point . . . "When you're giving what you consider a class party, then you keep it with everybody in the room knowing everybody else. Maybe not knowing them well, but at least knowing *of* them. Power loves power. 'A' list people want to be seen at 'A' list parties." And it's true; we rate a party from the moment we walk in. "If you see Kirk Douglas, then it's a glamorous party. If you're scanning the room and zoom in on Henry—oh my God, it's the top of the line!" trills one social climber. But there are also those whose presence means the hostess is scraping the bottom of the barrel. "You have to know whom to drop," one high-powered hostess advises.

## The All-Important Afterwards: *Debriefing*

And so we suit up for evenings out, sailing forth to see what we can see—and then to tell it!

"The fun thing about partying in L.A.," one Bicoastal notes, "is that dinners and screenings tend to end much earlier. So you don't have to wait till the next morning to do the postmortem. Half the time you've barely gotten in the door before the phone is ringing. 'Well, what did *you* think?' a friend who was there will ask you."

About what?

"What people really discuss is bad behavior. Drunken insults made by famous economists . . . Actually, anything out of character. People talked about the fact that Robert Redford seemed a normal, pleasant-enough guy for months. They always said it with a smirk, of course," observes one intellectual.

" 'How did she look?' The minute that I've seen someone, the next question is always, 'how did she look?' " says one socially successful businesswoman. "Now I'm not in fashion, so they don't expect labels; what they want is my readout on the whole gestalt. They're taking both her temperature and mine."

"People want to hear who always comes and never leaves," a socialite suggests. "They also love dishing whoever didn't fit in . . . in fact, I sometimes invite an 'odd couple' just for the fun of trashing them later."

"It isn't who's there, but who *isn't there* that really interests me," explains another.

"The fun thing about those gang-bangs for four hundred is that the guests can still keep wondering who's invited even after they've all arrived!" a popular extra man observes.

An experienced socialite explains how to deal with a touchy situation: "Say you have a good friend who's giving a party people are talking about and your *other* best friend isn't invited. Last week I was expressly told by one friend not to tell the other and —wouldn't you know it?—I was on the phone with the second woman and *she* asked if I wanted to grab an early dinner with her the day of the party. I said, 'Gee, I'm busy Sunday.' That's where a code goes into effect. We both understand that when one of us says, 'I'm busy that night,' the other doesn't ask, 'Oh, going where?' "

What should you do when *you're* the one excluded?

"Grace under pressure, darling. Be totally generous. Even offer recommendations. If a friend has ten in to dinner, he just can't have me every time," shrugs one gossip gamesman, "but I don't fancy him having thirty-four and not inviting me!"

## It's My Party and I'll Pry If I Want To

**Hostesses are the unacknowledged legislators of our words.** From the moment they start selecting and seating the guests to the time when wined, dined, pumped, prodded, and pampered we protest undying love, and kiss-kiss good-bye, our hostess has exercised continuous subtle—and sometimes less than subtle—control over our lives and conversation.

"If you really want to know what's going on, you have to give at least one dinner each week where you have only eight to ten," explains one practiced hostess. "That way you're not losing your guests' best in a dozen *tête-à-têtes* at other tables."

**The mix of mouths is all important.** Another hostess explains: "If you want to gossip, invite two or three people that you know will start things rolling; then you just sit back and listen." Your contribution is putting the right people together. And the smart *host* never has to appear a gossip—one somehow rarely suspects straightmen. Yet few such men go in for serious entertaining.

"Most conversations are started by women and ended by men. Surprisingly, 'liberation' hasn't changed it. Wives bring their husbands together; then she's the one who passes on what she picked up last night when he was busy repeating his favorite story," another hostess explains, waving a Perrier-laden maid my way as we chat in the sun-drenched salon of her Eastside townhouse. "Believe me, when you're new in town, what you may *want* is a man, but what you really need is a woman defender."

## Them That Has, Gets

"If you're willing to spend your money to entertain, you can always keep up with the news," observes one beauty who spent bundles of her husband's. "Power attracts everyone, but while you have to have money, of course, money itself doesn't get you into society unless you give it away. You have to become a philanthropist. Spend it on your friends; buy yourself a seat on a cultural board. Then suddenly you're in the know, sought out, consulted. And once in the know on anything, you're suddenly considered an expert on everything," our savvy socialite explains Better yet, don't just hand out your money. If you set up a small foundation, giving just half a dozen yearly grants, you can spend a lifetime feasting on the anticipatory gratitude of thousands. Gratitude, it has been observed, is the warm feeling occasioned by the lively anticipation of *future* benefits.

Whatever your card, be it charity, the arts, or politics, the best way for *you* to make it is to take another person/product/cause under your wing and get people talking about *them* (and increasingly turning to you as the source of inside news on this hot new item). All work and no play may make Jack a dull boy indeed, but for the advanced gossip gamesman, "working" one's playmates while playing is as natural as breathing.

## Black Tie Tupperware: *Word of Mouth*

> For all the Athenians and strangers who were there spent their time in nothing else but either to tell or to hear something new.
>
> Acts 17.21

**Something new.** Not only is there your *intime* antinuclear dinner for eighty, your smart little "give what you can" lunch for Senator Gary Hart, or super art dealer Mary Boone's gala opening for her latest discovery, there are also all those parties meant to promote not people, causes, or long-term careers, but simply specific products. One invites and lavishly entertains opinion makers so that they will "talk up" whatever perfume, picture, or pox you are about to release on an as-yet-unsuspecting world. Out is the upper-class taboo against higgling, while what *Town & Country* calls the "Black-Tie Tupperware" party is "in" with a vengeance.

## Hearts and Mouths

"The whole thing is knowing people and understanding their connections," explains one active New York publicist, kiss-kissing cronies with *Everyone* on either coast and both sides of the Atlantic. "There's an alcoholics' grapevine, a gay grapevine, a bankers' grapevine, a bookies' grapevine—even a new parents' grapevine. Haven't you notice how you can walk into a gathering of five hundred with the mother of a three-year-old child, and two minutes later you see she has almost magically discovered the only *other* mother of a three-year-old within miles and they're happily chatting away? Yachtsmen, fashion people, tennis buffs, art collectors, closet queens—they somehow all spot each other, and even if they've never met before they talk as friends, are up on the same gossip so if you make the right connection, with just one phone call you can get the entire circuit buzzing."

"You have to get the 'right people' interested and talking. But the right people are different for each kind of launch. It isn't like it used to be when there was one group of 'opinion makers' and they all sat around Elaine's," says another successful publicist whose words were echoed by several colleagues.

"I always call up a big gossip in the group I'm after and ask them for advice," another publicist explains. "If you make them feel they're the very *first* to know, they'll alert their friends without your even asking. People want to know what's up before it appears in the *Times*—that's what being really 'in' is."

But it's not just finding and chatting up the "right" people. It's your credibility as a source of "inside" news that gets people talking. (Indeed, "credibility" is a word almost as popular with publicists as with politicians.) How does the publicist maintain the credibility of his dish when his listener *knows* he's being paid plenty to say that his client's latest release is the most exciting epic since *Gone with the Wind?* Of course no self-respecting hack actually believes all the publicists' blather, and yet . . . Word-of-mouth launches are a bit like viruses: one is exposed to and unaffected by many; still, when the infection "takes," it's Saturday Night Fever.

"When publicists talk about maintaining 'credibility,' they actually mean just one thing: *Never* lie about the guest list. Never say Jackie O is coming if Lee Radziwill only said maybe," explains one social veteran.

"Names are the first and last word in the promotion business," observes the woman who practically invented polite PR. "And pretty basically the same old names. I could dream up the most inventive launch for a new car, have girls popping out of the glove compartment—who could care? But if I have Fred Astaire tapping on top as it's being slowly driven in—well, *My God!* Sure, cleverness counts too. It's always good to be able to give a harried style reporter a witty quote. But really, everyone is starved for glamour. If I promise Brooke Shields, you just know they'll all show up to see her—and later *talk* about having seen her."

Are grown-up, cynical, sophisticated "opinion-makers" really so star-struck as all that? Of course! The biggest glamour groupies are the glamorous. After meeting Pete Hamill and asking, "Who was *that?*" Linda Ronstadt was told, "He's such a star-fucker." "Oh, that's OK," La Ronstadt replied, "Im a star-fucker too." Or so swears one reliable reporter.

# 13 · Get Ahead as a Guest: Some Cocktail Strategies Explained

> The sole cause of man's unhappiness is that he does not know how to stay quietly in his room.
>
> PASCAL, *Pensées*

---

**First know who's coming to dinner.** Call ahead. RSVP yourself, and while you've got milady on the line get a bit of a bio on who's coming. But never ask for the guest list before accepting. (While a hostess desperate to have you might oblige, she'll avenge herself by letting everyone know of your pretensions.)

## Passepartout: *Here, There, and Everywhere*

> Though he be a fool, yet he keeps much company, and will tell all he sees and hears, so a man may understand what the common talk of town is.
>
> SAMUEL PEPYS, *Diary*

"Everyone calls this a 'relationship business,' " notes one successful movie agent, "but nobody has real 'relationships.' That's why you have to get out, make nice, and see who's changing partners. Sure, most of what you hear is dreck, but if just one time in ten a tip means business, I'm way ahead."

**Breaking away.** The Passepartout-style gossip is usually an agent, editor, inquiring reporter, politician, or some big deal's upwardly mobile first lieutenant. From the moment Passepartout hits the party (early), until the time he departs (shooed out with the extra help if there's not a better party elsewhere), Passepartout never sits down. (Except at the very last moment at a seated dinner. Even then, should he dislike his seat, he may slip over to "check in" on his date and, finding fate has dealt his fair a pair-of-Ace partners, he may just exile her to the "B" table in his place.) However rapt in conversation, Passepartout keeps scanning the crowd for promising new arrivals; then off he charges—ostensibly to "get another" or to use the facilities. Another useful ploy: Passepartout may suddenly wave greetings (to those he needn't even know) over the less desirable source's shoulder. In this case an urgent "Excuse me, I have to settle something with Jerry" beats the all-purpose "guess it's time to get another," especially as those being dropped may spy Passepartout making a beeline—not for the bar—but for the growing buzz around Jerry, Man of the Moment.

But such abrupt transitions aren't always necessary. The practiced Passepartout has an instinctive sense of party dynamics and "goes with the flow," first attaching himself to the receiving line, then hovering near the buffet tables until the shrimp, smoked salmon, and caviar are exhausted. Then, with predinner conversation klatches pretty well set, Passepartout often makes a gossip blitzkrieg—five minutes here, three minutes there: greet/brief/debrief/retreat—all four essential movements telescoped into a few concise queries and meaningfully dropped phrases. (Lest he lose his momentum, Passepartout "spots" some arbitrary soul he's "trying to reach" in the far corner.) Give Passepartout a hot item at the door and a crowd of hundreds will have the news just minutes later.

**The hand-off.** Any Passepartout worth the name can easily elude even the most tenacious talker. In the classic hand-off maneuver, Passepartout extracts himself from a bore's stultifying grip by introducing another into the conversation. Thus Passepartout makes a point of knowing everyone by name so that when in need he can always cry out, "Ah, Charles, have you met the fascinating Mrs. Ramsey?"

**Take her, she's mine.** A strategic addition to Passepartout's rapid deployment force is an attractive first mate he can leave behind to console the abandoned source and continue the interrogation.

**The art of the possible.** While some may *never* forgive your scurrying off after a livelier source, people are curiously indulgent of those who drop them for inanimate objects. Caught with a bore and need to cross center left to join the huddle of the century? Just say, "Look! Over there, isn't that sketch by Kokoschka?" while excitedly pointing in the direction you hope to travel. At which point *you* become a bore, babbling incoherently about "Expressionism," "Egon Schiele," and "Blue Riders," as you edge toward the sketch. (No Kokoschka but rather a trenchant primitive "Step-mommie," by the host's precocious eight-year-old now safely packed off to prep school). No matter. One glance, a swiftly murmured "my mistake," and you are once again your own man. This neat little pirouette need not be confined to sketches, but may be repeated *ad nauseum* with any number of silver-framed photos ("Oh, look! Isn't that John?"), dirty books ("Oh, look!), even the still-warm bodies of those who have already crossed the Great Divide into legend ("Marlene Dietrich!—you'll forgive me?").

Of course, even Passepartout doesn't always gossip in high gear. In rare contemplative moments he may simply plant himself midsalon at the point intersecting as many circles as possible. Or he may strike a pose beside some *eminence gris* and overhear the wizard's petitioners. Sometimes he even makes off for quiet corners. Stormy weather, he's listening in the library. Springtime, he's drawn to balmy terraces where the whispering breeze gets plenty of competition.

When it means making the rounds with the hors d'oeuvres tray, Passepartout will even play the helpful guest.

Is Passepartout a blackbelt in calculation? Is Ed Koch a New Yorker? But like the perfect hostess, Prima Passepartouts are born, not made.

## Tuned In: *The Art of Overhearing*

You don't have to be a Prima Passepartout to get an earful; just be an artful listener. After taking up the classic "listening-post" position at the intersection of several circles, let the talk wash over you as you scan the groups, matching up each voice with its owner. (This isn't half so hard as it sounds: for each half-dozen grouped together, one or two do all the talking.) The key is to keep scanning several conversations and then zoom in on hot items. It helps to know who's likely to have news. A good ear and sharp peripheral vision are also plusses.

One social light swears she can follow three conversations and actively engage in yet another! "I'm shocked to discover that most people can't!" she confides. Does she tune in to just a few key words? "No," she insists, "I can hear *exactly*." Whether or not you ever get quite so attuned, beware of others' acuity. That woman in the red dress two conversations away may well have heard your caustic comment on her *décolleté*.

But tuning in doesn't just mean wiping the wax from your ears. Like the practiced Kremlinologist, the nuanced gossip notes the all-important lines between the lines. (Why did your hostess draw you aside, and what, exactly, was the meaning of her exemplary story?)

## Holding Court: *Strong Silent Types*

> The power of remaining silent is always highly valued. . . . [It] is the distinction between those who give orders and those who obey them. Looks are the language of commanders. Even within their own sphere commanders tend to be sparing of words and thus one comes to expect of other taciturn men, when they speak, utterances which sound like commands.
>
> CANETTI, *Crowds and Power*

"The differences between those who sit and those who circulate is quite simply the difference between those who have arrived and those who are still striving," says one reporter. Just so, the senator stands his ground while his aides scurry. But success too has its degrees. While the prince holds court slightly off to the side, the king is enthroned way back in the far corner. (For the whole prestige of immobility lies in demonstrating how far out of their way you can make others creep to meet you.) You can always tell when a heavy-hitter is in the room by the stream of cutthroat counsels deserting their usual prominent positions for the Chairman's corner. There the whole scheming world brings its news; His Eminence's every remark is read as revelation. And if his response is only silence? Not to worry, the hustling young lawyer can still tell his client, "I talked to the boss about your problem."

## Becoming Somebody: *Or, "Who Is That girl? Haven't I Seen Her Here Before?"*

You are new in town. A stranger, but you are at least (thank God and your gene pool) absolutely stunning. How to break in? Should you hover at the edge of the group hopeful and ignored, while insiders dish intimates you wouldn't know from Adam? Hardly! Instead of trying to slip in, learn from those who have already arrived: set yourself quietly apart and let them come to you. You must look attractive, intelligent, slightly bored, and near oblivious to the party swirling round you. "A prop, like a drink, cat, or cigarette, can help," a former *Women's Wear* reporter notes. "But even then it takes great discipline to radiate quiet self-containment." Still, properly done, the maneuver works wonders. "People who wouldn't talk to you if you had *crawled* up to them will suddenly start whispering, 'Who *is* she?'"

When *they* initiate the conversation, the onus shifts; now they've got to prove themselves to you. Just be careful not to trip over the gossip passwords. "There was one lovely girl who had everyone interested until someone mentioned skeet shooting and she said, 'Yes, I just love skeet! She meant, 'to eat.' Well, you can just *imagine!*" my source declares over lunch at New York's Doubles.

## Outside Lines

> I have used society not to flatter my vanity or to humiliate them (I had other means of revenge . . . ) but, as I said, because they were useful to me and circulated about Paris on my behalf. Thanks to them I kept up with everything the way Proust, from the depths of his bed *knew what had been said at all the dinners* the night before.
>
> CHANEL, letter

But one needn't always play their game. To those whom He has already given much, God soon adds entrée. Indeed, if you begin to suspect you're even half a cut above "average," find your own turf and, once there, get down and cultivate your garden.

"The conventional wisdom is that you have to be out socializing all the time to keep up on what's happening in the business. That's crap!" says one brash young Yalie turned fast-track film executive. "I actually had an idiot working for me once who suggested we close the New York office during the summer and just entertain out in the Hamptons. 'Everybody knows that's where it's all happening,' she says. But just sitting around schmoozing doesn't create deals. A personal relationship rarely translates into action unless it's accompanied by professional respect."

Indeed, however charming and attractive your mother may find you, hanging on the edges of the In crowd not only steals time from the development of the project that will eventually prove your claim to fame, but also gives you a shopworn air. Far from always being a plus, simply knowing people can even work against you. (Asked why he rejected Proust's *Remembrance of Things Past* out of hand, the usually acute Gide shrugged and explained, "But, you see, Proust—I *knew* him!") It's doubly hard to see the greatness in a groupie.

"Because of the envious nature of men, it has always been no less dangerous to discover new methods and institutions than to explore unknown oceans and lands," wrote Machiavelli. If you don't "come out" until already a *fait accompli,* you can spare yourself much needless carping.

# 14 · Small Talk Is No Slight Art

> None of the desires dictated by vanity is more general and less blamable than that of being distinguished for conversation.
>
> DR. JOHNSON, "The Rambler"

"HE HAS no small talk" is hardly a compliment; "He that would please," Dr. Johnson explained, "must rarely aim at such excellence as depresses his hearers in their own opinion, for it is he who has stored his memory with slight anecdotes, private incidents, and personal particularities [who] seldom fails to find his audience favorable." While the intellectually insecure are forever invoking Disraeli's "little things for little minds," sages from Socrates to Sigmund Freud have been fascinated by the nasty nitty-gritty of existence. Though it may seem as if the occasional "all-business" type only wants to talk trade deficits or counterforce tactics, meet him halfway, and you'll suddenly find yourselves sharing fascinating bits about NATO screw-ups and export-import bank corruption.

But again, as with sex, so much is in the match. Give your partner only what he can handle. Let him decide whether he wants to steer for the deep or splash merrily about in the shallows. But don't let him tow you out beyond your range or you may find yourself embarrassingly adrift. (There *is* little worse than a Social Light trying to talk gene splicing with a Bionic Brain when her background is but a battered *Time* she skimmed at Kenneth's!)

Keep to your depth! (If you're not very smart, keep quiet. If you're very, very smart, keep *that* quiet too!) "A beautiful and sparkling but superficial woman rules a very wide circle," Goethe observed; "a woman of real culture a small one." So why pop an eardrum diving for pearls of wisdom? Like it or not, ours is a profoundly trivial culture. Let others strike pompous poses. "Just" gossip? Meaning is simply where you find it.

### Start Me Up!

> Curtsy while you're thinking what to say.
>
> LEWIS CARROLL,
> *Alice Through the Looking-Glass*

Don't neglect innocuous opening pleasantries. "You look presumptuous and familiar if you barge right in," one socialite explains. Perhaps the world's wisest mixer begins, "What do *you* think of . . . ?"

Another effective lead is "How do you know X?" (the hostess or whoever just introduced you). Always ask this before starting to dump. Press others for specifics, but keep your own answers offhand. You've either known your hostess "forever" or "she's a new acquaintance; isn't she *wonderful?*" Why pick either extreme? The better to start them up, of course! If you've known the subject "forever," your new acquaintance will assume you already know the dirt and not edit his or her remarks. On the other hand, if you've "just met" your absent friend, you're a *tabula rasa* ripe to receive impressions—and how many egos can resist a willing virgin?

Better still, personalize the standard "How do you know Jane?" by working in a bit about either party ("Do you know Jane from Vassar? from London?" and so on). If you know something about the subject that the speaker doesn't know you know (for instance, that Jane worked the streets of London), then your new friend's answer to your "innocent" question may well tell you more than she ever meant to.

Or, if someone of interest is within your line of sight, simply ask, "Who's that, over there?" While it seems gossipy to ask about absent others, even perfect strangers will answer your opening, "Excuse me, is that Jane Doe? with a helpful bio, should Jane be standing 20 feet away.

## Don't Hang Back: *People Love to Be Recognized*

> McTurk: Weren't you involved in the plot to assassinate the Prime Minister?
> Mayor: How *nice* of you to remember!
>
> JOE ORTON, *Up Against It*

Don't be shy and let the story of the second escape you just because you haven't been introduced. Step right up and ask all about it! Crisis and celebrity suspend social barriers. Fame? Infamy? What's in a prefix? John Dean still loves to talk Watergate. Fair or foul, it seems a fifty-yard run is still a fifty-yard run.

## Your Best First Move: *Flattery Will Get You Everywhere!*

> Thursday, May 26, 1921 I sat in Gordon Square yesterday for an hour and a half talking to Maynard [Lord Keynes]. Maynard said he liked praise; and always wanted to boast. He said that many men marry in order to have a wife to boast to. But, I said, it's odd that one boasts considering that no one is ever taken in by it. It's odd too that you of all people should want praise. You and Lytton are passed beyond boasting—which is the supreme triumph. There you sit and say nothing. I love praise, he said.
>
> VIRGINIA WOOLF, diary

Clever Virginia, to praise Lord Keynes by calling him esteemed beyond the need of praise! Honest, insightful Maynard! If not beyond praise, at least beyond pretending he doesn't need it. Whoever the man, whatever the season, your best opening gambit is praise. "We sometimes imagine we hate flattery, but it is only *how* we are flattered," the consumate courtier Rochefoucauld observed. Exacting brutes that we are, we demand not only praise, but informed praise. Thus, when we meet composer Jim Webb we mustn't gush, "I love your songs," which would only create embarrassed silence. Instead, start on a quieter, more specific note. "I've always loved 'MacArthur Park.' Tell me, which of the recordings is closest to the way *you* first imagined it while writing?" Even the modest Mr. Webb will reward you with the story of the song's inspiration, sales, and recording history. However, when you haven't done your homework, don't hazard a guess ("Oh, Mr. Stoppard, your *Homecoming* revolutionized modern theater!"), but merely smile, blush, and modestly lower your gaze as if suddenly confronting Divinity. While your betters deserve your best, even lesser lights ought to be offered intelligent openers. "Whenever I meet someone at a party and they say, 'Oh, what is it like to be a TV producer?' I just want the ground to open up and swallow *them*," explains one producer. The more discreet your fawning, the better, but if an occasional obviousness can't be helped, don't worry. When G. B. Shaw said, "What *really* flatters a man is that you think him worth flattering," he wasn't kidding!

## But Don't You Boast!

> It therefore comes to pass that everyone is fond of relating his own exploits and displaying the strength both of his body and his mind and that men are on this account a nuisance one to the other.
>
> SPINOZA, *Ethics*

We would rather slander ourselves than not speak of ourselves at all, Pascal observed. But often such self-slander is a none-too-subtle boast. Thus, the beauty bemoans her appearance while the genius laments his dullness. "This is a rather feeble joke of Henry's and we're all quite tired of it," the eternal hostess snaps. (Still, not so tired she would dream of dropping Kissinger from her "A" list.)

Nor is the outright boast much better. Never let word of impressive ties escape your lips, unless expressly asked. And even then, admit the connection with a modesty that implies you'd be more comfortable denying it. (After all, it's just a formality. Anyone with the slightest social IQ already will have made inquiries.) Similarly, keep your wits about you. Don't blaze your way to instant oblivion. People adore not those who shine, but those who help *them* shine more brightly.

But there is one boast we can make to great advantage: when others try to flatter us for some real coup we do well to shrug them off with a laughing, "Oh, it was just luck." Nothing seems more modest—or is more disheartening to our enemies. The opposite reputation can be killing, however. Once, a *petit fonctionnaire* came blubbering in to thank foreign minister Talleyrand for an assignment, tears of gratitude in his eyes as he explained, "This is the first break I've ever gotten." "What? Unlucky?" said Talleyrand, immediately withdrawing the appointment. Moral? Only report those stories that enhance your aura—not of ability (which others might resent) but of beautifully dumb, irresistible luck. Whom the fates adore, their fellows admire.

### Pass on Passing Judgment

"Let us start with something familiar to us all," Elias Canetti writes, "the *pleasure* of pronouncing an unfavorable verdict." A merely pedestrian work becomes the "bad" book of a "bad" writer whom we then decide is shallow, self-deluding, vain, and, it is whispered, impotent. "The pleasure of an unfavorable verdict is always unmistakable," Canetti continues. "[It is] a verdict pronounced with an almost unnatural assurance. There is no mercy in it, and no caution. We exalt ourselves by abasing others."

"As you get higher up, the gossip undeniably gets more vicious," one successful entrepreneur observes. "Is it because more is at stake? Or because players who make the final cuts play rougher? Beats me, but during the Twentieth Century Fox takeover the mud-slinging was rough even by Hollywood standards."

Yet even when fortunes don't hang in the balance, we often oblige our own—and our neighbor's—bloodlust. ("What do you think of Neil's review?" "Do you *really* want to know what I think?" we begin, winding up for our wickedest pitch. "Well . . .") But while much *is* undeniably mediocre, "average" is, after all, "par" for the course. "Those who have the capacity to abstain from judgment can be counted on the fingers of one hand," Canetti notes. Join this most select society, and hush!

But do lend an ear to others' critiques. Most reveal far more about the critic himself than he ever intended. Is the critic proud? Then pride is not so bad a sin. Is he bright? Then the brightness is all. Does he fancy himself well born? Then genealogy is fate. Fib as we may, our true beliefs will always out in the slant of our gossip.

## Don't Be Dreary

*Low:* I'm hungry. I need help.
*Mrs. O'Scullion:* I'm not interested in your private life.

JOE ORTON, *Up Against It*

To which one can only add (alas), "Amen." We fuss, fight, scheme, spend thousands on bugle-beaded Halstons, brave the muggers, our friends, and the elements in order to be amused, adored, and enlivened—*not* to face the hard truths. So put a good face on it. *Carpe diem*, darlings. We've all got grief enough at home.

## No Stories!

Every hero becomes a bore at last.

EMERSON, *Essays*, "Uses of Great Men"

There are many close calls in life and baseball, but whether you should take to telling lengthy stories is not one of them. While hard-news flashes ("Guess who just resigned?") or titillating tidbits ("Oh, didn't you know she used to live with . . .") have general appeal, set pieces slow things down. Your version of "How I Won the War" excites only your mother. No stories! Above all, no Collected Stories. The essence of good gossip is *intercourse*.

(Social intercourse, darlings.) I don't care how absorbing you think your holding forth is; remember, it was a storyteller whom Dr. Johnson decried as "not only dull himself but the cause of dullness in others." (Haven't you noticed the look of abject horror that flits over even your beloved's face when enemies suggest that, you "tell that funny story about your trip to Kenya" yet again?)

It's not just that brevity is the soul of wit, but that, as Voltaire observed, the secret of boring is to tell *everything*.

## Name-dropping: *Should You or Shouldn't You?*

> I am His Highness' dog at Kew
> Pray tell me, sir, whose dog are you?"
>
> ALEXANDER POPE, for the Prince of Wales' pet's collar

Many gossip in order to name-drop subtly. That is, they imagine it subtle. "I do it to impress the other fellow that I'm someone to reckon with," says one respected editor. "It has an instant legitimizing effect." But does it really? There are two schools of thought. Unlike my blue-pencil-pushing friend, I find name-dropping betrays an embarrassing need to impress. It's as if you admit up front you're not a very impressive piece of work and so must quickly compensate by introducing the names of more appealing others. Aggressive name-dropping also makes you appear a bit of a fraud. After all, if you're really so wonderfully bright and well-connected, why haven't they heard of you already?

Don't you drop first, but if your partner leads with a name, feel free to trump it. For example, your gossip partner tells a story about (and so implies a friendship between himself and) Tom Wolfe. You listen appreciatively, then ask, "Oh, yes, how *are* Tom and Sheila? Is he still reading nothing but Balzac?" and take the trick. (By name-dropping in the first place, your partner has shown himself the sort impressed by name-dropping.) When your abashed partner asks, "How do you know Tom?" you quietly answer, "Oh, actually I don't know him very well, really." True, but because you kept mum earlier, your partner will never believe you.

**Negative name-dropping.** If you can't resist indulging in an occasional opening drop, try negative name-dropping. Not "I saw Bob Dylan and he said, 'Blythe, you're looking fabulous,'" but instead, "I nearly *died* the other day when I ran into Bob Dylan and he said, 'Shit, Blythe, who do you think you're kidding with that leather jacket?'"

Certain subjects and buzz words are another sort of name-dropping. Talking about fluctuating exchange rates implies you're a globetrotter who makes and drops money in several languages. Ditto for detailed complaints about the world's top twenty airports. Still, as with all name-dropping gossip, get too far ahead of your audience and you lose the entire effect. Don't start a story about de Kooning when your audience's idea of genius is Reggie Jackson. (This is another strong argument for letting your partner drop first, so you can size up the sort of name familiar enough for him to know, but recherché enough to impress him.)

### The "Drop-Kick": *Or, "Get the Great"*

> Censure is the tax a man pays to the public for being eminent.
>
> JONATHON SWIFT, *Thoughts on Various Subjects*

Every news article must answer the questions "Who? When? Where? How? and What?" Good gossip must also answer the question "So what?" What easier way than by name-dropping with *your* news? Not name-dropping to impress but for the sheer joy of getting the great. "You know how I love Doris Day, but I'll never forget the time that Doris . . ." "I just adore Elizabeth Swados. Yes, isn't she a genius? Well, maybe not an *actual genius*, but undeniably a genius at drawing attention to herself . . ."

The most frequent object of the drop-kick in eastern establishment circles is Dr. Henry Kissinger. While one can reasonably be of many minds on this man and his works, everything, from where Kissinger vacations to his apparently insatiable money lust (his detractors haven't any?), maneuvers, and monomania, becomes grist to the rumor mill and sets him up for the drop-kick. "Did you read about Henry getting mobbed in Brazil last week? Well, Warren happened to be in town and when I talked to him last Thursday he said . . ."

Why get the great? "We worship them; then we destroy them," Susan Margolis-Winter, author of *Fame,* says of our idols. Mediocrity has no greater consolation than that genius is not infallible.

There seems to be a certain point of renown—call it "critical mass"—above which we will let few contemporaries rise without balancing the positive press with put-down gossip. (Perhaps the kiss of death for a media figure is a *Time* cover.)

Of course, not all those who "get the great" are jealous colleagues. Often people who scarcely know celebrities take a dump. Why? In order to appear to be an intimate. Familiarity breeds contempt; ergo, if I dump on "Woody" (Allen), "Henry" (Kissinger) or "Gay" (Talese), it will appear as if I know them. Such carping keeps to a few basic themes: he's greedy, he's a fraud, he has risen way above his level. How wicked the world has grown? Far from it! Drop-kicking is gossip in the classic tradition. "Detraction and spite find a ready audience," Tacitus explains. "Adulation bears the ugly taint of subservience, but malice gives the false impression of being independent."

## 15 · Who Wants to Hear What

*Tell me to what you pay attention and I will tell you who you are.*
ORTEGA Y GASSET, *Invertebrate Spain*

"You know, you really ought to do a scale, rate all the topics one to ten," one wit suggests. "Say, maybe, a rumor on a book deal is a one, an accurate inside trading tip is a six, and the *real* scoop on Brooke Shields's sex life is a seven!"

"You want to know what's the hot theater gossip? Whatever Stephen Sondheim's working on. You can never go wrong with *that*," sneers another critic. But while what Sondheim is doing may be a ten for show people, the Wall Street crowd couldn't care less. As always, good gossip is listener specific: while *Cosmo* girls worry about calories, playboys worry about cars, and *New Yorker* types angst over Connecticut property taxes. Still, mankind is everybody's business.

Belushi left every penny to his wife. Jack left Jill. The Von Bulows hadn't slept together for five years, and besides, Danish friends insist, "He was a total fraud; he just took the noble 'Von' and wasn't even a *real* Von Bulow." Such is the engrossing stuff of soaps—and people's gossip.

Actually, those who have come full circle, back to their childlike love of the merely amusing, are confident characters indeed. For most of us, however, the usefulness is all. As one tycoon told his wife when he cut short their first vacation in five years, "Every minute I spend on the beach I can feel them *gaining on me!*" While we're not all quite that obsessed with triple-lapping the competition, most of us doubly enjoy the tale we imagine useful as well as amusing. The irony of this, of course, is that so few of the "practical" bits we lap up have any real practical use for us. Still, we listen eagerly to news of great new shops we'll never visit and know all about people we'll never meet.

"Who's connected to whom? Who cares about what? How do they operate? Who underwrites them? To what tune? How can they best be approached—and rolled? When people "burst" on the scene, it pays to know where they're coming from," laughs a former Kennedy man who admits to a soft spot for old "New Frontier" gossip when not working. Indeed, it often seems like only yesterday from the way so many still enjoy dishing those now alive in legend only. Does such (often scurrilous) talk spring from love? Should King, Kennedy, Rockefeller, and Johnson kin be pleased or appalled by our enduring interest? (Perhaps a bit of both) When we can no longer talk *to* old friends, the next best thing seems to be to talk *about* them. Nothing beats nostalgia gossip, in its place, but unless you *both* go way back, better stick to the latest.

### Something New!

> ... —heaven or hell,
> Who cares? Through the unknown, we'll find the *new*.
> BAUDELAIRE, "Voyage", *Fleurs du Mal*

When modern man despaired of finding Meaning (God is dead and all that), he began to thrash about for something to assuage that awful gnawing feeling and so seized upon the cult of the new. Certainly any topic is enhanced by freshness. But so much is always "happening," that even all the *latest* isn't worth repeating.

How do we decide what's hot? Whose news judgment counts? Why, all the other gossips', of course! In a very democratic circular feedback set-up, we listen to what *they*'re saying to decide what *we* should tell.

**Flash! That's phenomenal.** Every so often someone is so very much "the latest" that even the smallest nonitem about him or her commands interest. Farah, Soupy Sales, and Suzanne Sommers each had their day. When Henry Kissinger burst upon the dreary Nixonian scene nearly a dozen years ago, he was an instant sensation. While no one but Jill St. John's press agent had ever cared whom she saw before Kissinger arrived, suddenly we all cared. No item touching Henry could be too slight, so long as he was still the latest.

But perhaps the best gossip is *new* news on the same old names. (That way we get both exciting change and reassuring sameness.) "Every day it's some new girl, but really, who cares?" shrugs one Hot Gossip. "But if Teddy were to have a major love affair, or if Pat Boone were to be picked up on morals charge—overnight, even passé people are once more *interesting*."

## The Mundane Sublime. Or, Jeopardy:
### Sad News Travels Fast

"You have to be in jeopardy to be a really hot gossip item," one socialite explains. "That's why we're always interested in people who've just split or are in some kind of trouble."

"Make or break situations, instability, when someone's in jeopardy or can put other people in jeopardy—that's when he's a hot topic," says another Top Girl. "That's why news on who is not getting his book out after taking a big advance beats talk about whose book is right on schedule."

"People only want to hear the bad news," one evening-news producer agrees.

"I call it 'fame by disaster.' There's a powerful blend of awe and contempt we feel for victims that lends them a certain fascinating radiance," notes journalist Susan Margolis-Winter.

"Whenever Katherine Graham fires the head of *Newsweek*, you never hear, 'Oh, there's this bright new light,' " says one Blonde About Town. "You only hear that Oz got axed. Now each time someone gets fired, somebody else gets that job—but is *that* ever the lead? No indeed! But by rights, if we were being strictly practical, the new boy should be the news since now *he's* the one whose favor we now must curry."

## Nothing Like Necrophilia

"He's hot. He's sexy. He's dead," ran the ghoulishly good-humored banner headline across *Rolling Stone*'s color cover photo of the late Jim Morrison. The active cults of Jack, Jim, Janet, and Elvis show that while dead men may *tell* no tales, they sure have plenty told on them! Some "fine and private place"! Hungry fans and *National Enquirer* reporters leave not even this last stone unturned—exhuming fallen idols for one final encore. 'Perhaps he isn't really dead,' whisper Morrison fans as, without even so much as a corpse, the beat goes on.

What else but death could have made Belushi even bigger? Such is the tantalizing lure of the great: if you "break on through to the other side" while still a star, the sky's the limit. Especially if you leave behind some loud-mouthed disciples (the Peter Principle). Next of kin also make for much morbid interest. When avant-garde Yoko Ono was coming out with a Grammy-winning album and married to a real *live* Lennon she only made the cover of the tiny, tatty, now-defunct *SoHo News*. But even many months after the tragedy, her photo splashed across the hardly *recherché Post* still sold newspapers (with the big news "Yoko Takes a Walk in Central Park").

## Juice

> Babies do not want to hear about babies; they like to be told of giants and castles.
> 
> DR. JOHNSON, Boswell's *Life of Johnson*

"There is nothing like power," one power-lover sighs, "even if it's only power remembered." Indeed, while reasonable men may differ as to which type of power is the most important and therefore most interesting, they never doubt that power is the world's eternally hottest topic. "People want to know how much money you've got, but they're usually even more interested in knowing who your lawyers are, because that's a quick way to see whether you're plugged into power," says one ace entrepreneur. And speaking of lawyers . . . "You'll excuse me?" he sighs, taking a fast phone call after giving a quick glance 'round to make certain no fellow Metropolitan Club members are seated within earshot.

"People who are rich are not necessarily big news," one socialite agrees, "but if you're powerful, it goes without saying you're hot gossip. Of course," she adds, "it's always that much better to be *rich* and powerful."

"Maybe we lawyers just have a more devious way of speaking," explains one smooth Harvard-groomed corporate counsel, "but here even the most trivial bit is treasured if it says something about the power lineup. The other day's hot item was about which partner had eaten the potato chips off another's plate—I *told* you you wouldn't believe it!"

Saint-Simon tells of an old courtier who said that at Versailles one needed a nuanced awareness of the latest power shifts because *"il faillait tenir le pot de chambre aux ministres tant qu'ils était en puissance, et le leur renverser sur la tête sitôt qu'on apercevait que le pied commencer à leur glisser"* (one must hold the chamber pot for ministers while they're in power and empty it over their heads the minute they start slipping). How little things change! We still start "dumping" the second we sense a shift in the balance of power.

## Power Styles

Talking power means talking power styles. "I like operational stories," mussed one gamesman, "stories that help you psych out the other guy's game: When do they sue? When are they bluffing? Which partner really calls the shots? How does he make his decisions. Are you in trouble if he gets back to you right away or if he takes a while to think it over?"

However big the deal, power gossip often turns on picayune-seeming details.

"You won't believe this," said Ford Foundation president Franklin Thomas, whom I was interviewing for a profile, "but people here even talk about the fact that I sometimes keep the blinds closed!"

"Oh, but I do believe it," I answered, "because every foundation employee I've talked to so far has mentioned it."

People who work in glass offices had better not close their blinds, especially if they're "outsiders" brought in to make changes. Smart power talk picks up on seemingly minor but enormously telling items. At first I couldn't believe it when, with everything from the economy to the fate of the Free World hanging fire night after night, D.C.'s cogniscenti would dish the day's latest installment on White House aide Hamilton Jordan's failure to return phone calls. ("Three days to get back to Tip O'Neill!") When, I wondered, will they start talking about the important stuff? But within weeks *this* newcomer, at least, saw that the gossips had already honed in on a defensive arrogance that would spell disaster on a world of issues. It's the little things that count—and are counted.

However, all power tales don't translate. While the powerful from one scene like to rub shoulders with the leaders from another, they often have very little to say to each other. Or rather, there's little they *can* say, since they don't speak a common power language. Thus, after one Washington whiz regaled the table with talk of "the Friday breakfast," "the Seventh Floor," the "secretary," and "the E ring"* for several revealing hours, an even bigger business type turned to me and asked, "Does he always go on like this?" Power may love power, but when it comes to talk, each keeps to his own balance sheet.

---

*"The Friday breakfast" was an informal cabinet-level Presidential breakfast. "The Seventh Floor" of the State Department houses the secretary and most of State's top brass. Similarly, the "E ring" of the Pentagon boasts the top defense team.

In fact, nothing is more boring that the "in" gossip of a group that doesn't speak your language! For example, one of the very hot topics in Washington is who's leaking what to which reporters. This is hardly a big concern in L.A., where one often *wants* to be known as a columnist's regular source. Capital types also spend more time talking about colleagues' lapel pins (pin color shows how close the Secret Service will allow the wearer to get to the president) than they may devote to all the rest of a man's apparel. But, again, such "hot" local topics are merely puzzling to outsiders.

## The Rules of the Game

> "I don't think they play at all fairly," Alice began, in a rather complaining tone, "and they quarrel so dreadfully one can't hear oneself speak—and they don't seem to have any rules in particular; at least, if there are nobody attends to them and you've no idea. . . ."
> 
> ALICE, dishing the Red Queen's set, in *Through the Looking-Glass*

We love to talk about rules as a way of playing out the power game. ("How dare she break that contract!" "He can't *do* that!") Big scandals turn on questions of what our set considers "good form," establishing a new norm until the next juicy crisis.

Juicy gossip about dry rules? Yes, indeed. Take, for instance, the celebrated David Begelman/Columbia Pictures check-forging scandal. As we know from Hollywood gossip, powerful producers are often a law unto themselves. So when studio hot-shot Begelman forged Cliff Robertson's name on a ten-grand check ("to be replaced"), the true scandal was that Robertson refused to play ball and keep quiet. For several tense weeks, Hollywood was abuzz—not over news of accounting fraud, as much an accepted part of the movie scene as gold chains on leathery senior citizens, but over the newsworthy outside chance that maybe, just maybe, the rules of the movie game were changing. Even when rules are not in jeopardy, few gossips like to use them as a measure by which to judge others and *find them lacking.*

## In Style

> A trifle consoles us because a trifle upsets us.
>
> PASCAL, *Pensées*

"Curiosity is only vanity. We usually only want to know about something so that we can talk about it; in other words, we would never travel by sea if it meant never talking about it, and for the sheer pleasure of seeing things we could never hope to describe to others," Pascal observed. Of course we don't just travel; we also buy art, have affairs, engage the famous, skydive, and ski in order to talk about it later. "You're where you should be all the time," Carly Simon sings to her vain friend, her account of his picture-perfect posing (what Freud called "the narcissism of minor differences"), the very essence of hot style gossip. ("Can you believe it, *artificial* flowers!" "Did you check that tan? Poor Laura! Doesn't she know *that* shade of terra cotta *died* with Aristotle Onassis?")

## Displaced Persons

> "MOMA Tower Accused of Playing Favorites"
> "Rents for Choice Spots Looking Foreign"
>
> Headlines from the two out of eight *New York Intelligencer* items on real estate, March 29, 1982

**Talking real estate:** While every man has his special art, sport, or fashion interests, we almost all talk real estate. Even buying brings no release. We still regularly wake up in a cold sweat alternately berating ourselves for paying the half-million (for two bedrooms!) and congratulating ourselves for buying in before prices went even higher.

Nor is this topic just hot "for owners only." By gossiping about the real estate market we can all work out displaced worries about the economy, inflation, and the anxiety-producing instability of things in general. Indeed, those not yet actually *in* the game often seem even more impassioned than the owners. ("What? She bought *that!* But the roof is practically falling in. Besides, it's not *that* great a view.") We clearly spend more time discussing "views" than enjoying them.

But while a man's home is still his castle, a man's home is, even more importantly, his caste mark. "What? Gloria was turned down?" we gleefully inquire. (Not that we bear her any ill will; it's just that we so adore speculating on the findings of that jury of our peers, the co-op board.) You are where you live. If you don't believe *that*, just ask a resident of Riverhouse, Bel Air, or the Dakota. In fact, the only thing we like half so much as comparing addresses is dishing each other's "interiors." Indeed, the "good" address is merely shorthand for the whole *House Beautiful* performance.

How do we know what we want? Why, by seeing and hearing what others have! Superagent Swifty Lazar keeps a lovely little Klimt etching in the front powder room, but not simply to make your pants drop. The stage is set so that you will talk about his wealth and art. (I own, therefore I am.) Talking other people's objects helps us get a handle on the owner's act. "Things of no use are endlessly satisfying," noted Colette. And, we might add, endlessly revealing. Just so, depending on the context, "Joan always has fresh flowers" tells us reams about Joan's tony origins —or pretensions.

"Those who laugh are always right," Chanel once observed. However numerous the offenses perpetrated in the name of style, rest assured, not a *one* goes unreported! ("Could *you* live with five different patterns of chintz in a twelve-by-eight-foot studio?")

Machiavelli tells the story of a prince who, when shown around a courtier's lavish dwelling, smilingly turned and spat in his face, explaining (with a wave of the hand indicating the tapestries, brocades, and mosaic floor), "I wanted to spit in a place that would offend you least." While only warlords can risk such directness, ridicule of acquisition-mania is the most common strain of style gossip. We want to know not only who's well dressed but also which heiress prostituted herself how for that one extra Armani jacket. We want, in a word, to know about fetishes.

## Object Relations: *Just Tell Me What You Bought!*

While we love dishing others' acquisition gestalt, it must be admitted that each clique of enthusiasts finds its own thing endlessly interesting. Thus sailors spin sea yarns, cooks chat Cuisinart, and collectors compare each other's *objects d'art.* While it's fun to dish what you could do without, be sincere about the big things. Never affect disdain for that which you obviously covet. Similarly, don't pretend to scorn money—but neither should you make too much of it. (Cling too fiercely to the gold standard and friends might think you have no other.)

"I'm always fascinated by little things that somehow reveal a man's character," says Bella Donna. "It could be the most *minute* thing, like that he kicks his dog, beats his children, or, sin of sins, never picks up a check. I've often heard *that* about people before I've even met them." The rich wouldn't enjoy their little meannesses half so much if they only knew how much their friends loved talking about them! Not that we don't also like panning profligacy. Has Stewart Mott's name ever been mentioned without heralding laughter?

## Talking About Taste: *The Heart of the Matter*

> Unlike the Cartesian man of reason, the man of taste has no principles by which he governs his actions. His is an artistry which has not been learned, for which he himself cannot account, and which others only clumsily imitate. . . . [W]hile the man of taste needs to follow only his own convictions, such men of taste are rare. . . .
>
> KARSTEN HARRIES, *The Meaning of Modern Art*

Those lacking innate good sense needed a standard of taste and so, Professor Harries notes, the "pseudo-ideal" of "good taste" was born. We jump to her dictates more slavishly than the aging playboy spoiling his last mistress, our enduring belief that *"le style est l'homme même"* insuring such spectacle will continue. Advanced taste talk doesn't stop with clothes. It also strafes life-style and intellectual fashions. While total trash has a nice alienated edge, cringe we must before mildewed homilies. I don't care *what* Chairman Agee did or didn't do before marrying Mary, but I do know that any man who could, in the midst of such scandal, sit down with a *Times* reporter and, with a straight face, recite Rudyard Kipling's "If"—*well!*

But we not only talk about others' taste, we also class ourselves by the taste of our talk.

### Is Sex Still Hot? *Take It with a Twist*

"People are interested in strange bedfellows of any sort: the boy wonder with the wrinkled wallflower, the society matron with the radical feminist," observes one very social animal. "But again, I think it's less a sex than a life-styles thing. We're all incurably into other people's arrangements."

"We don't really talk about sex in any detail," one entertainment lawyer insists, "beyond, if someone comes in absolutely trashed, saying things like 'Boy, you really must have had some night.' Sex is more often discussed by the secretaries."\* But while this may be true even of entertainment lawyers, it sure doesn't hold for the rest of "show business."

When they're not talking "deal" or "money," I'm told, even in mixed company our Hollywood friends get down to giving detailed accounts of who gives what to whom how well. "All anyone ever talks about is sex, drugs, and jogging," sighs one fast-track film exec.

But, to be fair, there's sex gossip everywhere. While small-town matrons may go on about "that tramp's morals," Tinsel Town talks her technique. "Sure, with men it's sex; sex is *the* great topic," one respected news producer almost salivates.

---

\*For more on office talk, flip back to Part Three, "The Pleasures of Your Company."

"Power is sex; place is sex; deals are sex. But the real turn-on, of course, is *actual* sex, the whole fantasy aspect of how and where someone whom you all know was seduced. Something a little different. Once on the way out to cover a Queens story, one newswoman climbed in the back with a sound man and they fucked all the way out; she climbs out, fixes her hair and makeup, does her little—pardon the expression—'stand-up,' then climbs back in and they're at it again, all the way back. (The punch line was always 'she got gaffed.') Now that was the big jerk-off story at NBC for nearly a year. I heard it from over a dozen different guys, some of whom even claimed to have been part of the famous crew, but I couldn't swear to you that it actually happened.

Is sex gossip accurate? While people consistently underestimate the sexual activity of the less than gorgeous, same-circle talk of current affairs is often right on target. It's the loose talk about quick hits in the past and speculation on other groups' affairs that tends to be misleading.

## People Are Talking About . . .

> Heroes are created by popular demand, sometimes out of the scantiest material, such as the apple that William Tell never shot, the ride that Paul Revere never finished and the flag that Barbara Fritchy never waved.
>
> EMERSON, "Heroes"

Often, what people are talking about tells us not so much "what's happening" as what people are curious about, afraid of, or ready to believe is happening.

"Knowledge is power"—if you buy this you probably think "truth is beauty," too. The relation of knowledge to power is far from simple, but having "inside" info sure gives the reassuring *illusion* of control—and often impresses the hell out of our friends, even if we still can't affect outcomes one iota. While all media purport to be first with the inside story, some private eyes spy more scoops than others. The more specialized a magazine, the more clearly delineated and "with it" its readership, the more likely a magazine will be to break or even create news hot enough to discuss. In two very different worlds, both *Aviation Week* and *Women's Wear Daily* can spark insider talk, whereas fan magazines count on their readers being absolute outsiders.

**Fame.** "Show biz may be a hot topic for some, but unfortunately I'm not very interested in show biz because it's too common," shrugs one socialite. "There're so few socially acceptable celebrities!" laughs a veteran manager. "Of course, ty gossip is just the most boring gossip in the world," snorts a power-lover. *Unless* celebrity anecdotes offer a new (and human) angle. "I was in Jerusalem filming and sitting in the King David hotel lobby waiting for an uncle of mine who was then in the cabinet, when who walks in but Liz Taylor and John Warner, honeymooning. She recognizes Jim and comes over and then she and I start to talk. Somehow the conversation turned to a film of mine on modern poets and she begins to reminisce about some reading Burton did of Dylan Thomas. How wonderful it was: his resonance, his feeling, his fire, his talent. All the while poor Warner is just standing there, looking lost. We were all feeling real embarrassed for the guy. It's his honeymoon, for Chrissake, and she keeps stalling starting upstairs. Still she *was* beautiful—fat, but beautiful—and absolutely spellbinding, rambling on and on about Burton. Finally, there's this big clatter and all these troops pour into the lobby, automatics at ready, and who are they escorting but my uncle! 'Well,' she smiles, 'I'd better go. I hate being upstaged by reality.' And with that she exits. But I tell you, after her, everything else was anticlimactic!"

People also really *do* talk about perfectly scandalous news items. Who could resist a story that starts with the farcical headline: "Headmistress Murders Diet Doctor in Scarsdale Love Triangle"! Similarly, once New Yorkers discovered their then governor's new lady had . . . uh . . . *miscounted* former mates, we not only talked, some of us even sported bumper stickers reading, "Honk if you were married to Evangeline Gouletas-Carey." Wilbur Mills's Potomac swim with stripper Fanne Fox, the Moral Majority's own congressional cruiser Fred Bauman—both occasioned "inside" comment. Until you get caught it's called "boys will be boys"; once you're hoisted by your own peccadillos it's called "having a death wish." Indeed, it often seems that insiders gossip about cronies who get caught, not to give you the scoop so much as to distance themselves from the unlucky one and reassure themselves, "That fool got caught, but I won't."

## The Sense of an Ending: *When "Shockers" Don't Shock*

> The attraction of a certain kind of explanation is overwhelming. . . . In particular, explanations of the kind "This is really only this."
>
> WITTGENSTEIN, "Lecture on Aesthetics"

"My absolute favorite gossip reveals when things aren't as they seem," one diamond-hard beauty explains. "We're always looking for the kicker that grabs you," one news producer notes. But we don't want something we can't handle. We all love surprises, yet hate being truly surprised. Half the enormous joy of gossip comes from its effect of "civilizing" chaos. What might have struck us as a nasty shock (he was *really* gay and she was still seeing her old lover all along!) becomes but another reported citing of that Loch Ness monster known as "the world." He found her letters and she had never really loved him (of course); her lawyers checked the books and discovered his whole empire's built on fraud. (We knew it all along.) Horror becomes incident, betrayal a commonplace and suicidal despair the stuff of witticisms.

All good gossip is an ironic unveiling. We make life a little more manageable by sharing and trivializing the turns it plays us.

Such talk also reinforces our own credentials as survivors. *We know the score.* "You can't fool me," every interjected "precisely" seems to say. "Isn't that just the way it goes now," says our slyly knowing smile. Of course he was. *Exactly.*

# 16 · Psyching Out Social Gossip

*Oververification often ruins a good story.*
BENNETT CERF

WHILE the office grapevine often gets it right, most "personals" offer far less reliable intelligence. The same goes for rumors in what we call "gentleman's businesses," "I have a little wisp and then I make up the rest," shrugs one entertaining editor who turns a more convincing tale than most. Indeed, one is often amazed by the obviously inaccurate, even internally inconsistent, fables intelligent adults blithely repeat between mouthfuls of dry-roasted almonds. Amazed, that is, until one recalls that gossip is a highly variable compound of news *and* entertainment.

"I believe everything and nothing," remarks one pol. "I believe it all unless it's patently mean-spirited," says a friend who had just confessed to making up most of his own stories!

While it's a far from scientific survey, most of my sources suggested eighty percent as the proportion of casual talk they thought *un*true. By contrast, studies show some kinds of shoptalk to be ninety-percent accurate.

How to weigh what you're hearing? A lot depends on who's doing the talking. "It's recognizing someone with reliable dish and reliable values," says one oh-so-social executive.

Reliable values? Yes, indeed. Implicit in your accepting the report that Jack acted "disgracefully" at Jill's the other night is the presumption that you and the speaker share a common definition of what constitutes disgraceful behavior for Jack at Jill's—no simple construct. (Is he perhaps an ex-husband or lover with special privileges? Does Jill keep a somewhat madcap, punked-out, or a rather *comme il faut* salon?) But what exactly is *comme il faut* these days, when all sorts of tricks can come out of the closet—or, to repeat my hostess's telling election-night query, "Who are *we*?" Whatever our informant's informing moral-aesthetic grid, we want to be briefed by those secure enough not to pick up on just anything and run with it. "Doris Vidor was probably the greatest society 'reporter' around," one Eternal Hostess recalls. "Her report on Rita Hayworth and Ali Khan's wedding was so funny! Doris always got it right down to the flowers!"

Barring intentional falsehoods, items tend to be more accurate when the person talking really knows (as Doris Vidor did) the world of which he speaks. But only too often we tend to talk not about close chums (they might take it amiss), but about precisely those whose secrets we're *not* privy to. Thus, ironically, our most lasting impressions of others often spring from the gossip of those who don't know them well either! The same high ego involvement that makes for accurate shoptalk is often absent from the social realm—as are opportunities for double-checking and penalties for passing bad information. Besides, at the party we often lend half an ear to several conversations and so may honestly mistake *which* famous Barbara (Streisand? Howar? Walters?) the man behind us said was "unhappy and switching" (production teams? men? faces?).

What psychologists call "the sleeper effect" also argues against accuracy. This simply means that over time we tend to disassociate the news we've heard from its actual source. Thus, you may tell me something about your worst enemy that I discount at the time as "sour grapes." Nevertheless, if I hear something vaguely similar a few weeks later I might volunteer, "Yes, I've heard something to that effect." (Now where had I heard it?) And once we repeat something ourselves, we tend to believe it.

"Don't forget the absolutely innocent screw-ups in translation," one jet-setter warns. But even sticking to English, social chatter changes as it moves along. A remark originally offered as pure speculation ("perhaps he's depressed by the market") is often picked up and repeated without qualifiers, but with embroidery: "Have you heard Peter's business is failing? He suffered heavy losses in the market." When several days later we again hear the sad tale of Peter's woes, we may no longer recognize it as the (amplified) echo of our original off-the-cuff remark. Ah ha, we think, so my first guess about Peter was right on target.

Sometimes gossip's entertainment value so predominates we don't even care if we get it right—nor do our listeners. "If I hear a story I know is false but it's too good *not* to repeat, I'll still pass it on clearly labeling it someone else's story," smiles our Blonde About Town. "If I hear something dubious but *wonderful*, I still repeat it saying, 'It isn't true, but it's funny.' Of course, they always believe it anyway," the Eternal Hostess chortles.

What is it about certain dubious tales that so excites our interest? The Royal Wedding sparked endless off-color stories. While the *Star* assured its readers of Shy Di's virginity, a savvier international set was trading royally prurient speculation on the secret sexual preferences of the entire Windsor family. Why in God's name would a journalist plugged into satellite feeds of the latest coups and catastrophes invariably open conversations (later to range over everything from telecommunications antitrust to Lebanon) with yet another was-he-or-wasn't-he? Because it was far less dangerous than dumping on associates, and far more interesting than talking about the weather. It's also a prime example of the Law of Inverse Accuracy: quite simply, the likelihood of an item's being accurate bears an inverse relation to the difficulty of checking it out. Thus, gossip on which couples have split tends to be more reliable than word of one partner's "secret" sexual preferences. The first corollary of the Law of Inverse Accuracy is, of course, that the likelihood of any item's being repeated (C, for circulation) equals the item's timeliness *(T)* times its interest *(I)* raised to the power of its liberating unverifiability (here, small *v*) minus any reluctance one might feel repeating it on the grounds of small $t$ (that is, taste). So we have $C = (TI)^v - t$.* This simply means that people (even the most sophisticated) like to talk about and feel themselves a part of "it."

"Oh, but the English are nothing compared to Californians," a veteran producer insists. "Out in L.A. they take the slightest bit and blow it up into a three-hour production. Everyone pretends to know even the most intimate details. You just have to laugh and say, 'How do you know? Were you under the bed?' Even that doesn't stop them! They come back with 'Oh, but darling, she's my *closest* friend.'" Perhaps such Wild West whoppers are a legacy of the old tall tales tradition.

## Keeping Up Appearances: *The Discreet Charm of the Bourgeoisie*

"I don't think that personal gossip here in the East is any less misleading. It's just different," one WASP volunteers. "Here, if you go to the right schools, join the right clubs, and 'play the game,' people won't talk. One of my father's friends was right out of an Auchincloss novel, did everything right—quietly smashing career at Brown Brothers Harriman, kids at Andover and Yale, nice little well-dressed wife who drank quietly at home instead of lurching about town—but the guy was a squash-playing Roman Polanski. I fancied myself quite the young stud when at Choate, only there wasn't a girl at Rosemary Hall he hadn't gotten to before me! Certainly in my family's set you can get away with much other people may even know about, but nobody 'talks' so long as you keep pushing the right image buttons."

**Watch your attitude.** It's not the deviant act itself so much as the spirit in which it's committed that sets people talking. Are you helping others overlook your "lapse" or flinging a glove in the face of convention?

---

*Because of the inherent inexactness of any calculation in the social sciences, logarithmic interpolations need not be carried past the third decimal.

**THE SCAPEGOAT SYNDROME**

Enjoying jailbait is one thing if you're a Lacoste-shirted investment banker and quite another if you're the foreign-born director of lyrically perverse horrors. The flip side of society's indulgence of its own is its abhorrence of those who thumb their noses at it. "Better to be vile, than vile-esteemed," chirps the Bard. And so it seems. Take the case of the late, great, much-reviled Lord Byron. Why much reviled? He was no stranger to either sex, but that's hardly news said of an Englishman. And surely other Romantics have fled their wives and fancied their sisters? Yet while Wordsworth and Dorothy quietly kept house, all England was after the perverse peer. Because he not only "got" it, he flaunted it, and thumbed his nose at polite society.

**Lord Byron's Law: No slanderer more vicious than polite society scorned!** Once caught out in one sin, rumors of others will multiply, the first scandal "proving" subsequent rumors.

## I Doubt It

> "One doubts on specific grounds. The question is this: how is doubt introduced into the language game?"
>
> WITTGENSTEIN, *On Certainty*

**SUPERNATURAL SELECTION**

**Will wonders never cease?** Apparently not. Some innate love of the miraculous tends to make even the cynical give more credence to more extraordinary stories! ("He couldn't be making that up. It's just too preposterous!") Perhaps we believe more because we want to repeat more; whatever the reason, tales of extraordinary doings travel faster, farther, and wider than more ordinary stories. (Indeed, Tacitus gives high praise to vanquished emperors who killed themselves in striking ways so that word of their death spread swiftly, sparing needless battles.)

**How big? Larger than life!** Few "sensations" are very sensational. In fact, we so hate so-so stories that we tend to inflate our appraisals: entertaining flicks become "masterpieces" and bumbling cutthroats "monsters" or "men of vision." When weighing others' words, remember that "supernatural" selection favors propagation of the fantastic over the merely factual.

## What's His Angle?

People often act as propagandists less concerned with getting specifics straight than with selling you on a larger "truth"—as they see it (or would like to have you see it). Correct for refractions by factoring in the speaker's angle.

**The waves.** Just as every man has his *idée fixe,* so eras also tend to go overboard, finding a Bolshevik under every bed or, more recently, a bisexual *in* every one. Be doubly leery when you hear that "everyone's doing it."

Also, beware of people who bring you news of problems for which *they* "luckily" have solutions. "Once I was up visiting a friend's family compound in Maine and one of the other houseguests was a young lawyer on the make. Well, not so young anymore," one style editor recalls. "We all had a pleasant enough time, but then, back in town, the strangest thing happened. That rabid social climber calls our hostess and tells her that he had heard I was 'planning' to write a nasty piece but that *he* had managed to have it killed. A total fabrication! Luckily, I was close to the daughter so they believed me, but isn't that rich? He didn't even dislike me. It was just a way he thought he'd get more 'in' with the family!"

While the pyromaniac fireman is a classic type and the tactic of talking a nonevent into a crisis to become a hero resolving it is recommended by pop power psychologists, Machiavelli wouldn't touch it. And neither should you. Such talk is offensive, ignoble, and sure ultimately to catch up with you!

## The Limits of Skepticism

> I really want to say that a language game is only possible if one trusts something. (I did not say *can trust* something.)
>
> LUDWIG WITTGENSTEIN, *On Certainty*

But enough paralyzing uncertainty! There quickly comes a time when we must simply go with our best bets. "Doubt itself rests only on what is beyond doubt. . . . [A] doubt without an end is not even a doubt," muses our dear Ludwig. When *you're* in doubt about a bit of gossip, take the following rules into account:

**Extract the adjective.** Uncertain about a rumor? Whenever you hear two or three different anecdotes boiling down to the same essence, extract the adjective and bank on that. Is the subject supposedly arrogant? headstrong? vain? cheap? fawning? None of the incidents may have occurred exactly as reported: still, the subject must be doing *something* to inspire the same reaction in so many others.

**Even as we speak.** Adjectival analysis is strengthened by the "even as we speak" rule. When someone says to you, "Do you know that she is secretly . . ." (a foot fetishist or whatever), no matter how often you may hear the tale (and following our supernatural selection rule, the more bizarre it is, the more likely to be repeated), the likelihood of accuracy decreases in inverse proportion to the subject's fame and the speaker's distance from the subject.* Some "secrets," however, are really less secrets than quietly common knowledge. In which case we sprint along the scale from the highly unlikely how-could-anyone-possibly-know secrets like necrophilia (after all, dead men tell no tales) to the fairly reliable "open secrets" (in essence if not in instance). All the way at the plus end of the accuracy scale is the "even as we speak" rule: gossip about repetition compulsions is always true. Chain smokers smoke; those reputed to be alcoholics invariably love their liquor; slobs are sloppy; cheapskates sweat blood when

---

*Discount less should the speaker have a specially privileged position (he serves as valet/boyfriend for instance).

they have to pick up checks; and a rake is a rake is a rake. It's almost a point of honor. (I have never met a man about whom someone said, "Oh, and he'll make a pass at you," who didn't.) The *modus operandi* makes the man.

Similarly, distrust those who pretend to take your interests more to heart even than you do. "Telling on" absent others is such a cheap way to score points with present company that such "warnings" are often pure fiction.

"I trained Truman not to, shall we say, 'fib' to me—but it wasn't easy," the Eternal Hostess explains. "He would get on these kicks: 'Oh, so-and-so is saying this about you but I really put *her* down.' He so harped on the viciousness of a particularly harmless friend I finally invited him to lunch at the old Edwardian Room saying I was also bringing someone I was sure he'd just be *dying* to see. *That* whetted his appetite. Well, I made a point of arriving late, and he was sitting at one table—and she at the next. He didn't recognize my friend, the 'slanderer,' because they had never even met!"

## Standards of Evidence

> The difficulty is to realize the groundlessness of our believing.
> LUDWIG WITTGENSTEIN, *On Certainty*

In gossip, there is no such thing as inadmissible evidence. Hearsay ("Alice told Steve that Anne had heard John was planning to . . .") and conjecture (Bob is missing and Carol is missing; ergo, Bob and Carol are off somewhere together) that would never be admitted as evidence in a court of law are part and parcel of gossip, which makes it seem awfully unreliable stuff until we remember how much "hard" fact begins as hearsay. Like the news, like government announcements, like what you read in the history books, like what your parents told you, gossip draws on many, varied sources, some better, some worse, some intentionally misleading, some honestly mistaken, others right on target. (Indeed, we need only read studies on the inaccuracy of eyewitness accounts to pray that our own liberty never hangs on such an unreliable reporter! Yet we value this above all other testimony.) Of course, you can't take gossip on faith, but, as for that, what can you?

# PART FIVE
# EXPERT

# Hard-Core Gossip Gamesmanship (Handle with Care)

# 17 · Ask and It Shall Be Given

*I have enquired after you, as after a new fashion.*
CONGREVE, *The Way of the World*

---

WHATEVER your goal, knowing what's in the wind will help you steer your best course: unload that overpriced commodity, step into that soon-to-be-emptied top spot, etc. But whether you're going to bank on it or simply repeat it, you have to get the gossip first.

The smart gossip will always listen rather than talk, ask rather than tell, and when asking, he will sometimes ask straight out. The question then becomes, whom to ask?

## The Source

Great sources are often those whose business is, quite literally, other people's business. Thus, reporters are excellent gossips and the best financiers are as handy with rumors as with numbers. But, according to one accomplished gossip, "Lawyers absolutely blow my brains." And news picked off the legal grapevine isn't privileged.

Anyone who needs to impress with his clientele will, of necessity, be a gossip. Boutique-owners, decorators, designers, maître-d's, real estate agents, even society doctors serve and tell. Salespeople in exclusive shops will urge you on with tales of who else bought those $400 slacks ("Diana Ross bought six") or keep you guessing which tycoon bought two pairs each—for his wife and mistress.

Masseuses and hairdressers offer intimate bits. Decorators will tell you how much each client spends. With a little prompting, you can even learn which rich husband is so cheap that his wife has to pay; and which "other woman" has the bills padded, taking a cut off the top for herself. If properly stroked, maître d's will let you know that your former partner dropped in the other day and, for a few dollars more, will even divulge what was cooking. And, of course, real estate agents are the first to know who's splitting and selling or who's looking for a little "extra" studio. (They even keep it listed!)

Don't be a snob. If you want political news, do as the senator does: ask his aide. The great gossip troves are often a level down. Whenever possible, endear yourself to servants and secretaries. Feeling wicked? If you show the slightest interest, your children's friends will tell you tales that Mommie and Daddy would die to have told. And should you sit up front with the chauffeur, there's no telling what you'll get. The walls are never thick enough.

## With a Little Help from Your Friends

There's a reason why high-powered people are always on the phone. The best way to hear what's up is not only to circulate yourself, but also to have friends on the scene, next to the water cooler, at the dinner, or in the key "principals only" meeting, listening for you. Later, you simply debrief them. But such soulmates are few. Far more often you'll be quizzing those who don't know what you need to know but still might have something of interest.

## Go Fish: *Or, "Just Tell Me What I Want You to Tell Me"*

For this vital little exercise we'll assume you have a willing partner. What we can't assume is that he's also telepathic. So slow down. The executive who thinks sixty-second phonecalls are efficient is only fooling himself. If you want others to offer you news, you must, at least, give freely of your time. So relax. Stifle that desire to scream, settle yourself comfortably in your chair, and begin casting a wide net of questions.

For instance, say you're on the phone with a friend who often sees people of interest. When you ask, "What's new?" she says, "Oh, nothing much." You then take the direct approach and simply say, "Well, go through the days (or nights). What happened at Monday's dinner. How was your meeting with the buyers?" Once you've given her the chance to recall where she was, you can also find out who else was there, what they talked about, who dumped what on whom, who didn't rise to defend a friend, and so on. Such systematic queries almost always turn up enough news for you to hone in on specifics and ask good follow-up questions. "Oh, Jeffrey was there ... Did he bring up the Stevens deal? Did Bonnie seem to agree?"

Unless your source is extremely busy, impatient, and important, the rule is, Ask, ask, ask! Like the good reporter, you just can't worry about wasting others' time. (But you can, and must, thank them profusely when you do take it.)

If your friends are smart, they'll often pick up on what you want without your explicitly asking. Whenever one socialite casually asks, "Did you see anyone of interest?" intimates immediately know she means her "absolutely loathesome" ex. "She wants to know *all* the details. When you last saw him, how he looked, and, most important, how he looked at 'the little nobody looking for a last name,' as she so charitably calls them," reports a friend. "God help you if she was gorgeous!"

## Advance Work

But what if—far from friends—those in the know are hostile, or at best indifferent? At one time or another we've all experienced the nightmare of being seated next to the perfect source, only to have what we thought our most ingenious queries met with silence or, worse, "You'll excuse me?" as off he runs. What went wrong? Odds are you neglected your advance work. The late Dowager Princess of Washington, Alice Roosevelt Longworth, herself renowned for brilliant barbs, let the reticent know that in her salon, at least, gossip was the *only* acceptable talk. "If you don't have anything nice to say, come sit by me," read the pillow by her side. The spot was never empty.

There is, of course, a great "home team" advantage to entertaining. The host not only picks up the check, he also sets the meeting's tone, time, place, and ground rules. The best gossip gathering atmosphere is usually one that fosters a feeling of relaxed intimacy. The best time: whenever your source is off his guard. Alcohol, overwork, fatigue, isolation in a remote place, distracting news, ill health, drugs, sexual attraction, and other pressing preoccupations all leave your source more vulnerable to a well-aimed question.

## The Relaxation Response

> Guil: Draw him on to pleasures—glean what afflicts him . . .
> Ros: We cheer him up—find out what's the matter.
> Guil: Exactly, it's a matter of asking the right questions and giving away as little as we can. It's a game.
>
> TOM STOPPARD, *Rosencrantz & Guildenstern Are Dead*

Your first aim is to put your source at ease. Never look worried or upset by what he tells you. Never make him feel guilty, embarrassed, or suddenly afraid he's telling you too much. Just heard that the illicit love of your life is also cheating with another? Ask casual-seeming questions now; cry later.

Similarly, if a big party or meeting is coming up and you see someone who was probably invited, ask straight out whether she's going. If you weren't invited, it's smart to say so immediately. It makes your source feel so superior she just may call you later with the scoop. And if she wasn't invited, she'll rush to reveal the "more exciting" something else she was "already" planning.

Another useful, somewhat more sophisticated variation of the relaxation response is *the inquisition.* Hold high-stress meetings, but ambush early birds for informal talk, then stay behind to "chat" with stragglers. Intent on watching what they say *during* the meeting, most people are quite careless about their talk before and after. Yet often an entire meal or meeting is merely prologue to a crafty lion's casual-seeming "Oh, yeah, I forgot, one last question . . ."

## I Only Have Eyes for You

One of the best ways to loosen up a reluctant source is to establish that all-important eye contact. *Don't* scan the crowd for something better. Fix his beady browns with your soulful blues. You'll be amazed by all he'll say when you hang on his every word.

"The eyes have it" cuts best across sexual lines; a beautiful woman to a powerful, self-absorbed man; or a pretty boy to an older woman (or man) of means. But "eyes" also works well whenever the listener is attractive enough for his source to be flattered by his attentions.

## The Fairy Godmother

> It was neither the sweetness of their [the sirens'] voices, nor
> the charm of their repertoire which riveted the passing voyager,
> but their profession of knowledge.
>     GEORGE STEINER, "Dante Now: The Gossip of Eternity"

The older woman tends to give "the eyes have it" turn her own special twist. No longer quite the dazzler of former days, she throws in a little something extra. The way she greets you at the door ("I've got a little something for you," *sotto voce*, Cheshire-cat smile), implying that she has been on the phone all day on your behalf. If only the material lived up to the teaser! But alas, the "little something" she offers is often just that: the same trifle she serves as news *du jour* for all her intimates. For she'll take not only *you* aside; if you watch, you can see her go *tête-à-tête* with your mate and the ten most important guests who came in after you. Yet, for the privilege of entering her "charmed" circle she'll demand you surrender up your every secret!

## Meet the Wizard

The best way for a senior gossip to find out *everything* is to set himself up as oracle. (You confess your sins in the hope that he can keep you from having to pay for them.) Only a select few can use this near-effortless technique. Such souls radiate the soft glow of enduring success. They are shrewd, sharp, calculating, and so well connected that their pull almost ensures their forecasts' accuracy. "Well, how can I help you?" the wizard asks, his attentions so soothing you never notice his probing for more important clients.

Be advised: if you need a wizard, save up twenty dollars and consult an astrologist. His advice will be just as trite and true, but at least he won't know whom to tell your secrets!

## Point Blank

> If a person has no delicacy, he has you in his power.
>
> HAZLITT

While it's great to ease news out with "I only have eyes for you" charm, those in the know aren't easily seduced. Indeed, the rich, powerful, and bored are often those who have seen, heard, and *lived* every story. How does one engage the blasé? Be outrageous! Ask them what no one else has ever dared to. For instance, if you simply ask some self-made men, "Are you rich?" they can't resist giving you a full accounting. But know your man. Point-blank questions are for either the truly vulgar or the very sophisticated.

Such questions work best when asked in a bantering "are you man enough to answer this?" manner. Play with your source, but don't let him play back. If he nevertheless manages to return a point-blank volley, smile and say, "You know, sometimes I wonder that myself." Or simply laugh, throw your hands up, and exclaim, "Don't ask!" Remember, point-blank questions are hot and so they should always be handled coolly.

Questions on the topic of the moment are best asked point-blank. If someone has just been fired or lost his magazine, you can bet he's secretly dying to talk. So be supportive. Stand by your man and he'll give you the whole blow-by-blow account—*his* version, of course. But once you hear his side, you can check it out later.

Humor also helps. Let your source know that you think his woes are just as silly as he'd like to believe them. "Do you need carfare home?" one clever woman asked Norton Simon chief David Mahoney after the board had cut his massive salary. Mahoney smiled; then Mahoney talked. "People always open up when you validate their denial," our source comments.

## Show and Tell

This gambit works best on secret show-offs and the none too brainy. "Give me five words that describe you," you say, and mouse that he is, he starts out, "Diligent, thoughtful, hard-working . . ."

"No," you interrupt. "I see you don't know how to play the game. Let me go first and show you. I'm ambitious, grasping, snobbish, loose, and vain. OK, now it's your turn." And he's yours. However large the party, the contact between the two of you is suddenly intimate. Besides, you've gone first. Once he has heard *your* secrets, he can't back out. (Of course, your "secrets" are only slightly blacker words for the nasty things everyone is already saying.) But caught unawares, *he* just might let slip a true revelation.

## The Direct Approach

Parties are the best place for the direct approach. The atmosphere is supposedly nonadversarial and most people have been drinking. The only place better than the crowded salon is the back seat of the cab you're sharing home. They'll be dying to share their impressions, and moving from a larger to smaller group often lends the illusion of safety.

The direct approach can also go out to lunch, on a first date, or getting-to-know-you drinks. Part of the deal is that you must at least appear forthcoming on the latter two occasions. But lunch can also prove dangerous: once you're seated, you're stuck. Yet who would refuse an invitation from anyone, even an enemy, provided he was interesting!

## The Seemingly Direct Approach

When confronted by a woman, Mafia associate, financial adviser, brain surgeon, or other cautious types, it's often best to take the seemingly direct approach; that is, ask innocent questions about one thing to learn about another. Something as simple as, "Where are your kids going to school?" yields a wealth of socioeconomic data. If you think a marriage is breaking up, ask, "Is it true you're selling the apartment?" or "Have you taken that lovely house for next summer?" or "Are you and Jerry ever free for dinner?" If you suspect they've just lost their money, inquire about vacation plans, or ask her to join you shopping. A wife's going back to work or school also can be the tip-off to divorce court or financial disaster.

## Trust, Loyalty, and Other Scouting Virtues

Whenever possible, start your digging with a show of concern. "Poor Jan, how is she?" or "Steve is such a genius; has he found the right job yet?" Another easy way to show concern: simply put down your source's enemies: "Carl was such a snake; how *is* Anne these days?" But be careful. If you really don't care, or can't act, a show of concern can backfire.

## Flattery Is Disarming

Preface your questions with disarming phrases such as "I hear you give the most wonderfully relaxing weekends!" or "Aren't you *the* bright young director?" and you can ask them almost anything. But do your homework. Specific, well-aimed compliments are essential.

Clever flatterers also use the trick that helped make PR whiz Ben Sonnenberg a multimillionaire. Always tell people the good things you've heard about them—even if you have to make them up! Attributing your flattery to another still warms your source while making you seem less the flatterer.

## Not-so-free Association

Simply mentioning his rival's name is often a great way to get your partner going. (Even strong silent types say plenty if you bring up someone who dropped them.) You can also learn much from what others want to dodge. If conversation with your dinner partner is going swimmingly until you mention another man's affair with his secretary, odds are your companion is having one with his (or that his wife is seeing hers). The advanced gossip may mention bankruptcies to a man she suspects is in financial straits or tell adultery anecdotes to the wife of an alleged philanderer. Press bravely on despite their pain. Don't expect a full confession, but do catch that fleeting "God spare me" look. Words may lie; expressions rarely.

## The Buddy System

> Trust not yourself; but your defects to know.
> Make use of every friend—and every foe.
> ALEXANDER POPE, "Essay on Criticism"

You can learn what people think of you simply by asking friends to "just mention my name." (You need a thick skin for this one, because you can hear back much worse than an icy "Oh, the *dear.*")

## Horse Trading

Sometimes you have to give to get. If you can't wheedle windfall gossip, trade for it! If you don't know the caliber of another's talk, start trading slowly! ("It's been a busy season . . ." "Did you see that piece about Perry? He doesn't get a percentage of gross." "No kidding. *She* doesn't either?")

Don't get greedy. It should never be obvious that you want more than you're willing to give. If trading with another pro, deal straight from the hip. One grande dame of New York gossip wastes no time laying it on the line. "I've got something good for you," she coos, "if you've got something good for me."

When delivering hot news, brief is best; then cut quickly to your listener's reaction.

## Silence Is Golden

Once they start talking, keep your mouth shut. Indicate interest, but don't interrupt. Even when they pause, you needn't pick up. Don't be afraid of silence. Dead air, particularly on the phone, will prompt your partner to keep talking.

If your source isn't holding back but really running out of steam, though, help him along. "What did Steve say while all this was going on?" If he says, "I don't know about Paul; I have nothing to say to him anymore . . ." and then hesitates, give him permission to dump. Nod, murmur, "Yes, it is strange about Paul . . ." He will go on.

## In Extremis

There are times when you don't just want information, you desperately *need* it. Someone may be angling to acquire your job or company. Or perhaps a nasty divorce is pending. If your spouse has also had flings, you'll survive; if not . . . The time is clearly right to cross-examine sources.

Take everyone out to lunch and go over everything, step by step yet again. While one generally shouldn't ask friends for information it might cost them to reveal, sometimes the stakes are such you simply must call up and say, "Look, if you feel you can't tell me, don't, but I think you know something I *need* to know. Can you tell me about it in the strictest confidence?" This usually works in the crunch. If, however, your friend does let you down, just ask for the name of someone else "who might be able to help," letting your friend off the hook gracefully. Then she'll spend the rest of her life feeling guilty, grateful, and trying hard to make amends by telling you absolutely everything!

# 18 · Seek and Ye Shall Find

> To see, be seen, to tell and gather tales.
> ALEXANDER POPE (paraphrased from Chaucer)

WE don't always hear the news. Sometimes, if we're alert, we actually *see* it happening. With armies of informants round the globe, Houston-based gossip columnist Maxine Messenger still insists she gets her best bits "going out with my own little body." One smashing scene is worth a thousand stories. You may have *heard* that Faye Dunaway was difficult, but *seeing* her storm away from the next table is believing. If, as Henry Miller writes, the brave man is one who says, "it happens here," then the smart gossip is one who adds, "and you can bet I'll be around to watch it."

Look sharp! Serendipity is where you find it. We've all run into newsworthy doubles in Central Park. But all odd couples aren't adulterous. If you catch TV stars racing through the St. Regis lobby at contract-renewal time, trust me, their assignations with network execs are all business. Shopping for stories? "Stumbling" upon interesting news is a question of being tuned in: of knowing *where* to go *when* to see *what*.

**What's in Store:** *Confessions of a "Personal Shopper"*

What Georgetown's social Safeway is to Washington's power elite, Giorgio's boutique is to Rodeo Drive's rabid consumers. Go listen to the stars complain. Watch them fight with their men. Why settle for *Scruples'* consumption à clef when you can see the same show live, *without* the names changed!

But Californians don't have all the fun. Back in New York, what off-track betting is to bums, Bendel's is to trendies, while Brooks Brothers suits the eternal preppie and his sister. Just as we all have chums we're bound to find in certain bars, there are others whose voices we're sure to hear ringing through the dressing rooms at Bloomie's. That people who work and play together should frequent the same stores is no surprise; what *is* surprising is that they don't think of this themselves and at least look around before discussing colleagues.

"I know it's dumb to talk," one lunching lady groans, "but how was *I* to know her dearest friend was also in the dressing room, lurking just behind the next curtain?" Men are spared such temptations by their more open approach to fitting and their wise habit of shopping solo.

## Does She or Doesn't She? *Only Her Hairdresser Knows for Sure*

Men are also spared the beauty trap. While dressing rooms can be dangerous, beauty parlors are a potential disaster—in part because they *seem* so safe and cozy. Remember, little snippers have big ears. (Just because you can't even hear yourself doesn't mean that everyone within thirty feet of you doesn't catch every word when you take calls under the dryer.) Calling your broker during your regular wash and set is a case of flagrant overtipping.

"It all happens here. I get the stars here. They do the deals here. Big deals. That's *J*-o-s-e, *not* Hozay!" the short, plump hairdresser (whose own brown tresses stream to the small of his back) announces, as if he were God's gift to women. Perhaps he is. Didn't Jose snip and streak Farrah to stardom? Doesn't Jackie Bisset swear by his ultra-chrome Beverly Hills shop? And look, isn't that Ali McGraw sitting cross-legged under the dryer?

Indeed it is. But the aging ingenue draws not a glance. All eyes are on two fast-talking ladies butting rollers over a sketch-filled notebook. A row of leggy beauties raise their expensive blonde heads from the rinsing basins lest they miss a word, but Jose waves them back down. "Sure, whether they're switching agents, parts, or lovers, I'm always the first to hear," Jose confides. But there's no more time to talk now. The lady Jose is "doing" clamors for his ear. "You see," Jose explains picking up a comb as she continues her monologue, "they need me. They trust me. That's Jose," he calls after me. "J-o-s-e."

I laugh, but back in Manhattan my own inscrutably oriental Miwa has only to smile and say, "Ah, so good to see you," before we're deep in conference on our five hot topics: men, yen, sex, society, and why my hair is always such a bother.

Of course, hairdressers aren't the only ones who understand. Charismatic faith healers of all sorts hold semiprivate confessionals while ostensibly teaching everything from aerobic dancing to Zen. And speaking of healers, society doctors' waiting rooms are gossip goldmines. "It's half the reason I go for treatment. I met Mr. Ludwig the other day—you know, as in the richest man in the world? At this point, I sometimes wonder if I could afford *not* having back problems," one gamesman chuckles.

At the salon, on Rodeo Drive or in the waiting room, part of the checkout is being sensitized to who (or what) might appear. Each specialist has his "specialty." Top cardiologists get killers like Greek shipping magnate Niarchos. East Side diet doctors and endocrinologists see, slim, and comfort the already svelte likes of Lynne Revson, while Fifth Avenue pill doctors shoot up Seventh Avenue stars and their whole speedy entourages. But Park Avenue plastic surgeons' waiting rooms are the real school for scandal. (Isn't that little Gloria behind those big shades?) No names around when you look in? Dr. Lookgood will whip out his polaroids to show each famous nose before and after.

"Doctors drive me crazy. It's always 'I capped Cheryl Tiegs's teeth. I did Lassie's hernia.' I call it dropping credits," says one veteran TV producer. Back East, name-dropping doctors play a smarter game: dropping wealthy clients' names to draw even richer ones from whom they hope ultimately to extract large status-enhancing contributions for New York Hospital.

## Closely Watched Planes

We're still the transportation generation, regularly hopping planes to inspect that site, close that deal, or make that assignation. Airports are, quite simply, gossip goldmines. And what reporters, revolutionaries and detectives have always known, businessmen are learning. One London-based firm about to make a Hong Kong bid sent a young MBA on ahead just to watch incoming flights for signs of the competition.

But it's more than just a question of who's hopping where. Airports also offer a juicy slice of life. Though evolutionists swear it all started in the sea, I, for one, believe that life as we know it began in the teaming, screaming rush of the modern airport. Overhear gents calling home to report delays, briefcase dangling from one arm, pretty pinstriped partner from the other. Then rush to the noisy shuttle lounge and eavesdrop as big-city power brokers compare notes on *Annie*'s opening, Abe's funeral, or the latest tax rulings. Hear them make hurried deals before you slip off to the mortuary-like stillness of the VIP lounge—only to be awakened by the famous final scene of last year's fun couple. Ah, the cries and whispers—hurried promises, parting shots, and fugitive warmth of last-minute embraces! I could watch forever, but they're paging my flight. And look! Over there, now isn't that . . . ?

And gossip-gathering opportunities don't stop at takeoff. It takes nearly a day to reach Tokyo and most have had it with *Years of Upheaval* by the time they've reached Alaska. Lonely, bored, increasingly drunk and desperate, some take silly, stand-up chances in the restrooms or make loud dates for later, followed by even more awkward confessions. Instead, sack out on long flights—alone. Partying on planes is sure to ruin your reputation.

## "Lost" Weekend?

Want to slip away from the world's prying eyes for a few days with a special friend? Before you spend a lifetime searching for that happy hideaway, let me save you the time. It doesn't exist (unless you own your own Greek isle—but if you're in *that* league you're also plagued by telephoto lenses). Yes, I know Conrad's heroes lost themselves in the mystic East, but such getaways are gone. I'll never forget my chagrin when, after island hopping in the East for days I finally landed in Bali and ran smack into the same old crew of junketeering senators. Whether you spend hours or days in flight, all too often the dreaded: "Why, hello! What a *surprise!* How *nice* to see you . . ." greet you on arrival.

There are certain places where the chic meet to retreat. Never take friends' advice on great little "out of the way" resorts unless you're looking forward to running into them on arrival.

"We heard of this great secluded spot so we took off, switched planes—the whole clandestine bit," recalls one social literati. "We finally arrive, peel off our sunglasses, and are sinking into this incredible beach's talc-like sand when a voice suddenly rings out behind us: 'And then David Obst said—!'" The voice belonged to none other than Lynn Nesbit, literary agent. Seeing that flight was impossible, our hero tried charm, so successfully that to this day Ms. Nesbit has not only kept his secrets, but also her ten percent as his agent. Here's to our friend's sangfroid. Even horror stories can end happily if you show the courage of your lack of convictions.

However far and wide you roam, it seems you're never really safe. Indeed, the scarcer your sort, the more that natives notice and remember. (They're *still* trashing Margaret Mead back in Samoa.) And restless natives aren't your only source: you needn't pump Haiti's Hotel Olafson owner Al Sykes to get the intimate goods on three decades' worth of visiting celebrities—he'll gladly tell all without your even asking!

Other important travel tips? When discretion is in order, never piggyback business and pleasure. Though the company pays for your fun, your associates are sure to notice your arrangements.

**Au! Restaurant!** So you want to be alone? Even in midtown there are select haunts always packed because we *imagine* them hideaways. Here waiters aren't the only ones who pick up tips. One film executive swears she paid for her beach house by cashing in on inside trading talk overheard in an East Forties walk-up called Pietro's.

"There was a time in the late sixties when limousines were double-parked around the block and I counted four Rockefellers here at a sitting. They knew they could relax here," one stylish restaurateur explains. "Once when Bobby Kennedy was in the photographers were waiting in ambush so we slipped Swanson out the back and the two of us walked out arm in arm! But it finally got impossible to keep things quiet."

"For all the talk of power breakfasts at the Regency, the really big-deal meals aren't out. Guys with impressive directors' dining rooms have a leg up keeping negotiations quiet," says one Wall Street Raider.

But business affairs aren't the only ones calling for quiet. Owe the mistress a meal? Wife out of town, but you're afraid all her friends are not? The obvious thing would be to drag your date dangerously uptown or slip off to one of those dark, illicit-feeling cafes in the West Forties. But such stops don't do much for morale, and if you are spotted, the jig is up. After all, why *else* would people like you be dining in a dive called Giovanni's?

"But people never tell," one erring husband insists. "After all, why are *they* there?" Poor fool. I hadn't the heart to tell him that dancing with someone else's squeeze stops few from naming other daytrippers they bump into!

"In Europe, it's easier. There a man brings his wife to friends' homes and takes his mistress out. Here it's just too dangerous," the silver-haired Italian sighs, explaining why "see and be seen" brightness now floods his café, once synonymous with tasteful adultery. "The wives get around—and the lawyers!"

Still, there are ways to beat the talk. If your friend is from out of town, just slip downstairs to the hotel dining room. Locals won't be eating there, and *should* someone see you, it's so un- speakably shameless, your meeting has *got* to be innocent! (Whatever your line, bring a briefcase to the table for added cover.) But don't risk this move at haute haunts like the Carlyle, where *everyone* hangs out. Or, if you're married on the European plan, find an elegant bistro slightly off the beaten track and clearly establish it as your extramarital territory. Once everyone knows, there's no point talking.

## "In" Among the Initiated

> "En 1824 au dernier bal de l'Opera, plusieurs masques furent frappés de la beauté d'un jeune homme qui se promenait dans les corridors et dans le foyers, avec l'allure des gens en quête d'une femme retenue au logis par des circonstances imprevues. Le secrete de cette demarche, tour à tour indolente et pressés, n'est connu que des vieilles femmes et de quelques flaneurs émérités ... car, pour les jeunes femmes qui viennent afin de pouvoir dire; J'ai vu; pour les gens de province ... [*l'Opera*] ... n'est plus compréhensible que la Bourse pour un paysan bas-breton. ..."
>
> BALZAC, "Une vue du bal de l'Opera," *Splendeurs et Misères des Courtisanes*

As Balzac makes clear (What? *You don't read French?*), merely to see is one thing, but to really "see" what's going on you have to be "in" among the initiated. Pity the poor rich man's wife; while hubby hunkers down to "real" work, she's often sent out to lunch as spy and proxy. "If you do lunch once a week at Le Cirque, once at La Grenouille, and twice at '21', between the maître d', your partner, and the people you see (and *overhear*), you're sure to pick up something," one such "working" wife explains. And if you look like our fair lady friend, you're also sure to spark some comment.

But lunching ladies aren't the only ones who work at seeing, being seen, and overhearing. Businessmen, actors, directors, writers, and artists also frequent restaurants they may *say* they loathe largely to have it said they're seen there. Or seen there *with*. Entering on the arm of a handsome friend may turn around the talk on Jilted Jane. Ditto for a faded star spied dining with a hot producer. See it at Elaine's, then read it in the next day's columns.

Why frequent Elaine's? Why court the bistro's slovenly madonna? Why, the very same reason maître d's are (very sensibly) courted the whole world over. While the food she serves may only be so-so, Elaine dishes the most tantalizing gossip. Just breezed back from the Coast? Need a quick fix on who else is around dealing, sleeping, or speaking with whom? Then head straight for Elaine's, pull up a chair, and, if you're a star, Elaine Herself may give you the rundown.

"The best way I can describe it," a former Nixon aide explains, "is that getting chummy with maître d's is like keeping up with the games you miss by reading the sports pages." But not all the action gets reported.

"If I'm here for something quiet, it stays quiet. But if I lunch with someone I want to be seen with, I can count on Walter to let news slip to the right people," one socialite observes, deftly cutting her cold chicken.

# 19 · Drive Defensively in the Fast Lane

> At the age of fifteen, when all instincts are still in their natural state, we can hardly believe that circumspection—that is, the art of revealing only a part of one's actions, thoughts, feelings, and impressions—is the most important of all activities.
>
> TALLEYRAND, *Memoires*

THE first thing that strikes the newcomer about talk at the top is how very *careful* everyone is: how little the cleverest people have to say. Even after the drinks have been refilled, *New Yorker* critic Michael Arlen broods silently, and Russell Baker, wickedly funny in print, sits dumb. In the center ring (offering not a word on himself or the recent dismissal of his network's president) Mike Wallace questions a trimmer Dr. Kissinger who, slightly miffed, declines comment.

So many achievers in the room! The very air aches with ambition. So many massive egos in such a dangerously small space. No wonder open attacks are almost unheard of in public. Regicide is not the sport of kings. While one should always gossip with care, in the fast lane caution is imperative. Talk at the top travels by Concorde. The stakes are higher; the information web is tighter, more invidious and efficient. So many eyes are on you. So many ears are pricked up, so many mouths poised at the ready, willing and able to fire off rumors that will be heard around the world, from L.A. to Paris, from Bonn to Barbados.

Entertaining indiscretions often rewarded in less lofty circles are despised as signs of weakness at the top. Supernovas need not spill secrets to impress you. Besides, why swap for items offered freely by associates and admirers? Even with gossip, them that has, gets—and for nothing. Tom Brokaw doesn't have to ask Dan Rather about his contract. Instead, Brokaw may be given the details by an NBC reporter who asked a news clerk who sleeps with a CBS vice-president. While some trading still goes on at the top, true give and take is hard between two heavies, both determined to do all the taking. Unless those trading "go way back," such talk is often nine parts posing to one part information.

For even at the top, one gossips above all to impress; one simply does it more subtly. "I was there" (with the president or at the hot party) is still the unspoken, but all-important, tag to every story. However, this lofty pose is not without its cramps. When tantalizing tidbits do come up, the poser is often trapped by his need to appear all-knowing.

## Don't Lead with Your Chin!

> To knock a thing down, especially if it is cocked at an arrogant angle, is a deep delight to the blood.
>
> GEORGE SANTAYANA, *The Life of Reason: Reason in Society*

Lead with your chin and you put yourself at the mercy of the group's gossip. One of the cruelest, most innocent-appearing ways of "getting" outsiders is simply to turn the conversation they have presumed to join to "coded" inside talk.

" 'All right,' " one power-circuit perennial challenged his bright young dinner partner. ' "Let's see if you *really* belong. Name every important man who ever had an affair with Pam Harriman." ' A hush fell over the table: did she know her way around? "Of course," my source shrugs. "I just reeled them off."

One example of how leading with your chin can make you the object of endless ridicule is the "grasping at straws" introduction. Legend has it that *Scruples* author Judith Krantz approached "real" author Tom Wolfe at a large cocktail party, gushing, "I'm so glad to meet you! You know, we have the same publisher." For one awful moment onlooking literati thought Wolfe's *very* up-market publisher, Farrar, Straus & Giroux, had lost their ... well, no one knew quite what to think until Krantz added that they had the same *paperback* publisher. (As there are only a few big paperback houses, almost all writers ultimately end up with the "same publisher" in this diluted sense.) Don't grasp at straws!

**Exception: get out your calculators.** When you're an outsider with nothing to lose and you know where you're going once you cross the Rubicon, march on! For example, when John Tyler, a widower, was president, actress Julia Garner was present at a ceremony where a gun backfired, causing panic—and inspiring her to swoon seventy-five yards and collapse into the president's arms. They were married three months later. Of course polite society could talk of little but the seventy-five-yard swoon for years, but in this case the actress had so much to gain that, as First Lady, she could afford to let them talk. After all, they still lined up for invitations to the White House.

## Watch Out! Your Feelings Are Showing

> The sage's consistency is only the art of keeping his agitation shut up within his heart.
>
> LA ROCHEFOUCAULD, *Maxims*

It's not just what you say but what you show; except with the Trusted Few, it's often in your interest to hide your interest. Not for nothing are history, fable, and everyday language rife with warnings against "betraying" our emotions. Why depend upon the kindness of strangers? Are you so uncertain of your self and feelings that you must instantly express them? However, emotion *can* be shown on behalf of friends: "I can't *believe* John is saying those things about you! I'm in an absolute rage!" Beyond that, however, most view all emotional displays (other than such culturally encouraged transferences as a "love of tennis") as "losing" and "unmanly."

Never frighten off your stories. "A casual snipe is fine, but people shut up if you seem *too* passionately interested," says one smart gossip.

"Don't get carried away with wild emotion," another ace gossip agrees, "because suddenly the story shifts. Last week a friend was on the phone telling me about another man we both deal with—but with a desperate edge. I mean, he was telling it as gossip, but I *knew* something was wrong. So I cut him off, saying, 'Don't tell this story to anyone else in the world.' He was startled. 'Why? What's wrong with it?' I just said, 'Look, we'll talk about it at lunch. Meanwhile, just don't tell this story to anyone, not in this way. You may not even think you're in it, but believe me, *it still makes you look terrible!*' Over the years I've developed quite a poker face; you have to."

## Squelch the Urge to Tell

> Mortals speak insofar as they listen.
> MARTIN HEIDEGGER, *Poetry, Language and Thought*

The smart gossip is selective. Never let high spirits, a third martini, or love of the story for its own delicious sake overwhelm more vital considerations, such as not appearing to be a gossip.

Respect your listener's antennae. Don't try too hard to titillate. Never take unnecessary exhibitionistic chances. You can dress your secrets up, but don't try to take them out. Consider the case of the tall blond radio personality who regaled her set with the story of how she and her married lover were almost caught *in flagrante* amid the egg rolls of an uptown Chinese restaurant. She pretended it was the tale of an unnamed *friend*—to no avail. Her "friend's" identity was only too obvious! Since everyone loves repeating the riddle he solved himself, the original-cast version of her story was soon heard at all the best places. Moral? You can't both keep and tell your secrets.

"Anything for a good story" is a fine motto for journalists, but the Fifth Amendment is more applicable to the trials of *self*-reporting. Of course, the danger is why some fast-lane types spin tales that turn on this razor's edge. All games of chance are thrilling, but reputation roulette causes real-life disasters, so why do it?

Gossip is *not* loose talk; it is instrumental speech: language in the service of power. Effective manipulation of others requires consistent self-control. Don't let a slip of the lip (Freudian or otherwise) sink your ship.

## All About You

> It is very disagreeable to seem reserved, and very dangerous not to be.
>
> CHESTERFIELD, *Letters*

Never spend more than the necessary minute giving news on yourself. You don't want them to hear. Still more important, nobody really wants to listen. That is not to say you should seem defensive. Always humanize your performance with a few seemingly intimate items. But after sketching in your basics, stop. The less you fill in, the more others will take for granted that they know you. Don't disabuse them of this useful notion. What they don't know can't hurt you.

There is no "idle" curiosity, at least not in the fast lane. If someone presses you for more information, suspect him. An old friend's renewed fascination with your affairs is often the tip-off to upcoming betrayal. Similarly, should your spouse show a suddenly rekindled interest in your every move, avoid self-incrimination by clamming up. Or, when on the spot, mumble, nod, repeat, spin long irrelevant yarns, put your listener to sleep. In short, when danger threatens, dare to be boring! Don't emulate the better half of the once-famous fun couple who, furious at waking up in bed alone at 3:00 A.M., waited up and greeted her errant husband at the door with the exciting tales of her own *Thousand and One Nights* of extramarital activities. He stood spellbound until dawn—it was one thing for *him* to, but how could *she?* Alas, unlike Scheherazade, poor, broke better half let her own stories get the best of her. While her confessions cut his ego to nothing that night, they did the same to her alimony a few months later. Never underestimate the awful potency of words—especially when the hour is late, the listener male, and the topic erotic.

While exes are a nuisance, admirers can be fatal, especially when the attraction is mutual. (If it's not mutual, get your "only kidding" signals straight from the start.) Black rumors begun by lovers scorned pale beside the creations of the totally frustrated. However, if you *are* turned on, and it's useless to resist, go ahead; just remember, oral sex need not include the whole sad story of your life. Your ship in the night may pass, but whatever you tell him will surely resurface.

When one is weak and exposed, the impulse toward verbal intimacy is nearly overwhelming. Even those who should know better have nearly finished themselves off. We know one savvy lady lawyer who would have taken a big client down with her had her talk not been stopped short by Lothario's snores.

But one can't always trust to fate. Use force of habit to shore up wavering will. Work substitute gratifications into a face-saving ritual: drag deeply on the philistine's postcoital cigarette. Get up, do stretches, take a shower, get out. If you absolutely must hang around and talk, call room service, the weather, the hour, or tell (don't ask) your partner how "great" it was.

The tender confidences exchanged during lengthier affairs are, alas, both more inevitable and inevitably dangerous. Today's lover isn't necessarily tomorrow's vengeful chatterer; it's just that the odds are good. Why take chances?

The easiest damage-limiting exercise is to refrain from lustful behavior toward members of your own set. If you simply can't find an obscure object of desire, limit your pillow talk to pants, moans, sighs, and nonsense syllables like "I love you."

## Learn How Not to Answer a Question

> Personal Freedom consists largely in having a defense against questions.
> CANETTI, *Crowds and Power*

The polite thing is to answer an innocent-seeming question directly.

Every day millions with good manners subject themselves to danger, humiliation, delay, and near-toxic levels of boredom merely doing the polite thing, but *you* certainly shouldn't. Since one often only sees what news a question was designed to elicit *after* the secret has slipped out, extinguish the habit of reply. Recondition your responses. Never answer even the most innocent-seeming question directly (unless you have a story to plant and have maneuvered your listener into asking). Remember, even responses simply reflecting your honest opinion often fall into the "dangerous" category.

The best response to an acquaintance's question, "How do you think Jane is doing in her new job?" is probably, "God, I've been too busy to even know how *I'm* doing, let alone worry about Jane," at which point (if you loathe Jane) you may purse your lips, act as if you're about to say something most interesting, but have second thoughts, and stop.

"What is it? Tell me," your listener insists, now dying for the answer to what was once a throw-away question.

"No," you hesitate, nervously lighting a cigarette, "it was just something I heard the other day . . . not the kind of thing you like repeating . . ." (See Chapter 22, "Character Assassination Explained" for "More Oral Sadistic Phrases.")

**Simply overlooking it.** First pioneered by recalcitrant children, then sharpened by the selectively hard of hearing, simply overlooking it is another smart way to beg the widest possible range of questions. Deceptively simple, it remains a favorite technique of both the child and the grand master. This ploy is the pick of presidents. Indeed, what politicians doesn't swear by the political variation—answering what they *wanted* to be asked after repeating or rephrasing the question?

But what to do in situations less obviously *sauve qui peut*, when the question has your name on it? Turn the question's apparent innocence to your advantage. Like the clever judge, construe the case so narrowly that you deal only with the surface and leave the larger questions still unanswered.

While follow-up questions are fine on "Meet the Press," straight out cross-examination is far too obviously adversarial for most social situations. However, the weaker of the pair may press the stronger when relations are supposedly cordial. Thus, a reporter may grill a public official and a woman laughingly press a captain of industry—up to a point. But open prying is offside and need not be dignified by any reply beyond a cryptic smile. Toss in a biting "Tell me, why are you so interested?" should you want to teach the offender a lesson. (But don't tempt fate by asking this of anyone given to offering outrageous comebacks.)

Of course, the best way not to answer prying questions is to make others afraid to even ask them. Let word get around that you hate gossip and nosy people. Then, greet all queries with offended silence as you continue asking "serious" questions. While such behavior might leave a poor man friendless, go right ahead and have it your way when it's *your* cook, *your* limo, and *your* smashing beachfront mansion.

If people aren't afraid to pry (because it *isn't* your party) give them something else to be afraid of. Become known as "dangerous when cornered." For example, should someone persist in quizzing you on how it felt "to be let go—I mean *actually fired,"* you might cut her off with a graciously smiling, "Getting laid off wasn't so rough; the important thing is to keep from getting intimidated by people who ask questions implying *they've* never been fired. But then, I'm not telling you anything you and Peter don't already know from your own "time off" last winter."

Somewhat less specific but equally "up yours" in attitude is the cut-off quip. When Nosy Nancy bares her teeth to approximate a smile and says, "Darling, I'm so very glad to see *you* here; I thought the two of you were separated!" then pauses, eyes glistening with synthetic sympathy, you simply smile sweetly and say, "So did I." Full stop. For the first time in her life she will be speechless and you will have found the line to get you through that last command performance.

The far side of outrageous is obscene. A former business partner keen on affecting the appearance of rapprochement grabbed one fair lady at a packed party and, grinning broadly, said, "Aren't you going to say hello?" thinking he had her cornered. But while word of the encounter shot through their crowd as he had hoped, the usually fair lady's reply was far from the forced hello he had banked on. (Unfortunately, we can't quote her exact words since the outrageous remarks' absolutely unprintable nature is what makes for your target's total devastation.) Few ask embarrassing questions once they've discovered *they're* the ones who might be embarrassed. A reputation for a vicious mean streak also serves as a powerful deterrent to those who might be tempted to slur you.

## A Slight Sensation

Our rule against autobiography still holds even should you find yourself co-starring in some scandal. At such times your side will be believed only by your trusted few, so give *them* the scoop and let them do the talking for you. (But don't retreat to some sunny hideaway. Leave the scene and others will feel free to say any wicked thing they like—or worse, to forget you entirely.)

Stick around; that is, unless you know that by staying you would bleed on the rug. While no one minds having drinks with the hypocrite who pretends to be aggrieved, real victims depress us no end. You further your distress, the more sincere your suffering appears. Far better to be known as "that bastard." Has anyone ever survived the epitaph "poor thing"?

The best way to ride out scandal is to hang in, keep cool, and not protest too much. Concentrate on appearing happy, rich, and fit. Men often doubt what they hear, Machiavelli tells us, but seeing is believing. Speaking of whom . . .

## On Advice: *You Asked for It!*

> Do not give advice to anyone nor accept any, except for general opinions.
>
> MACHIAVELLI, *Letters*

Stalled in love, life, or career? Rethinking your next move? Time to call your friendly colleague for advice, right? Wrong! Within twenty-four hours your confidant will have told the tale all over town, twisting your slight dissatisfaction into the most abject failure. Or so one Washington star discovered when he turned to a fellow newshound for a night of scotch and sympathy. Alas, it seems our stalled star's "friend" was so flattered to have been chosen as the star's confessor that he couldn't resist advertising this news—and a few of the juiciest items. These stories flashed from newsroom to newsroom as if wired. For days media backstairs were abuzz with little else but wicked quips on poor Carl's "what can I do for an encore?" anxieties. Remember, most "starfucking" isn't sexual.

Pity the falling star? With what he's seen of leaks, he should have known better. Asking for advice violates gossip's golden rule: *never tell on yourself what you would die to hear repeated.* While some imagine that asking half the town for advice gets everyone interested in their careers, being *interested in* hearing of your false starts is a far cry from *having an interest in* promoting you. (For that, you need not only bare your soul, but offer them a percentage.) So get by with just a little help from your *real* friends.

## Whom Can You Trust?

> I know you and the compass by which you steer.
>
> MACHIAVELLI, *Letters*

With gossip, it's less a question of what you say than of whom you tell.

Never trust anyone who tells you too much too fast, whether about himself or anyone else. He will be equally indiscreet in his handling of your news. But don't fall into the opposite trap of thinking that the strong, silent type will protect you as he does himself—a mistake, I blush to confess, even I made when, lolling in a hot tub by the sea with the tight-lipped tycoon, I thoughtlessly answered a personal question. It was not, alas, the only time the world would hear my answer.

Keep quiet in front of all heavy drinkers, pill poppers, and eccentrics with a macabre sense of fun (spelled s-a-d-i-s-t-s).

Never breathe a word in front of boring gossips, those tediously undiscriminating in-one-ear-and-out-the-mouth types who must tell all because they have as much air-time to kill as a twenty-four-hour news station.

Feel free to swap stories on a strictly confidential basis with major league sluggers only if you are ready to see your "confidence" in tomorrow's paper. Likewise, delight in the social moth's titter, but before you chime in, remember: they tell *everything* and *bitchily*. (You can never tell what the insecure will do with news when desperate.)

The best (most reliable) gossip is informed, yet discreet and secure, someone who doesn't have to worry about being invited back. Someone with his own very comfortable power base, well adjusted, clever, self-disciplined, and not overly envious.

Between the types who always tell and the Trusted Few fall the many for whom loyalty is very much a question of "it depends." So know your listener—and your listener's listeners. Know his fears, ambitions, and values. Discover where his interests lie; anticipate the route your news will take by keeping up on his associates and old and new-found friends and lovers. It's likely, for instance, that even a man who isn't a keen gossip would call an old flame to repeat the news he has heard on her. And as for present companions . . . Never make an enemy for life by asking "harmless" questions like, "Why did you marry your wife?" Indeed, take care not to talk (even jokingly) to a man about his current secretaries, wife, or lovers. God only knows what he will report back, but we guarantee it will be designed to make *him* look good and to make it seem as if *you* were the one doing the flirting.

Never speak in other than glowing terms about anyone whom you know your listener knows well and likes—or knows well and despises. (The story gets back just as quickly to either.) However well-intentioned your remarks, you can rarely be fawning enough to please. In fact, if you want to play it really safe, gossip only about those known *to*, but not very well known *by*, you. Class clowns, scapegoats, has-beens, and self-appointed great ones are other easy targets.

Absent friends are another story. Don't think someone is a safe mark simply because he's rafting down the Amazon. Nor are overseas friends dead-letter boxes where you can safely drop what's too hot to tell at home. One NBC correspondent reports that he was never so up on the latest at headquarters as during the two years he spent safely "tucked away" in Johannesburg, thanks to his many callers.

## Safety First

> Quod dubitas ne federis. (When in doubt, refrain.)
> Latin motto

Don't perform for the group. Save your lethal stuff for one on one where, if worse comes to worst, you can always deny it. Never even make sly remarks in front of more than one. Once you give gossip to the group it's open season.

Also be careful about situations in which it's just you, they, and maybe a tape recorder. Your opposite number doesn't have to be a spy with a well-wired olive; any microcassette will do. (The tape is admissible evidence in court even if you're recorded without your knowledge.) And tapes aren't the only traps on phones. His secretary might simply be taking shorthand on the extension. Also, beware of that slight echoing sound that announces you're addressing a group via speakerphone.

Another must in this Age of Xerox: never write a letter! (And never tear up one that you receive.)

Deciding not to gossip in a group is easy, but to whom can you turn for the all-important *tête-à-tête* where the real news finally starts flowing?

Talk to the Trusted Few, of course, but remember to expand your network slowly:

- Never trust anyone you've bought unless you've got them on a lifetime retainer.
- Remember the old Chinese saying, "Why do you hate me? I've done nothing for you," and don't trust those you've

helped up from so far down they'd rather that neither you nor they remembered.
- Conversely, be wary of your own former mentors.
- Never trust anyone who wants what you've got. Friend or no, envy is an overwhelming emotion.
- Phase out confidants who get into relationships with indiscriminate gossips or people who simply don't like you. Assume that even your Trusted Few tell their lovers all, but don't you do it.

Whom can you safely trust to use your gossip for and not against you? The pointers above give some clear-cut "don'ts," but in the end we must trust our instincts, far from fail-safe even in the shrewdest characters. Or so a man who was once youngest studio head ever discovered when, after telling tales out of school to a "friendly" reporter, he got not the puff piece he expected but a termination because of the article, which featured his jokes about the chairman.

Never expect a reporter not to print something hot regardless of the ground rules. (Or a gossip columnist not to make up what she can't find out.) In short don't expect anyone who could profit from using your information not to—whether he's a journalist, ad man, or broker.

Remember gossip's golden rule: If you absolutely don't want something told, then don't *you* tell it.

## Too Damn Hot

Sometimes over the course of a trying life, you blurt out things so very hot that even someone simply passing it along might get burned. Say one evening you're depressed and complaining so bitterly about your husband that your dinner partner asks, "If you're so unhappy, why don't you leave him?" Once you blurt out, "I am," you're lost unless you do as one rich man's wife did, adding the heart-stopping coda: "day after tomorrow."

By giving so terrifyingly much away, you suddenly throw your listener smack in the middle of a horrendously messy real-life drama. Audience becomes accessory. Once up for a scandalous earful, he has now heard far more than he's comfortable knowing. By telling, he would have to take sides (and responsibility) for upcoming changes. Good gossips talk *about*, but don't themselves become involved as anything more than behind-the-scenes players.

Don't bring people their bad news unless they're the most intimate of friends and they absolutely need to know. Even then avoid the appearance of having come to gloat by making sure the telling of this unpleasant information is an obvious favor: that the tipoff you offer your friend saves a deal or helps avert political disaster. Even then, let the teller beware—and have the evidence handy.

Think of all the brilliant careers and friendships ruined by laying things out a bit too straight. Is your friend really up to facing his troubles? Are you? Remember, bringing a friend word of his woes is an implied commitment to help him.

## Never Bring People the Bad News on Their Mates

> [The duke, on finding his wife *in flagrante*] upbraided her for her lack of discretion, "What if someone *else* had found you like this?"
>
> JEAN ORIEUX, *Talleyrand*

Never bring people the bad news on their mates. If they really wanted to know, they would know already. Almost everyone has eyes and a few hundred dollars to hire a detective.

The only possible exception: if separation talks are already on, you might offer a friend money-saving intelligence. But even then, proceed at your own risk. Many would rather pay than know. Force someone else's hand and he just may raise it against you.

Generally, unless you're a journalist, you don't want to become known for breaking bad news. (It makes you seem a scandal-mongering vulture.) Instead of spilling the hot stuff, simply keep up and, when the story finally breaks, come forward with the authoritative version.

"I'm talking about the world—life, art, politics, perhaps, but never gossiping," the smart gossip's every story seems to say. This blatant collective fiction works because your listeners don't want to appear gossips either. The following rules make the double fantasy even easier:

- Start by talking business (pronounced with a silent "gossip").
- Whenever possible, dress your hearsay up in facts and figures. ("They were married just three years." "He got a $400,000 allowance.")
- Ask serious, specific questions. ("What's the mandatory term for fraud?" "Did she sue in California?")
- Proceed with what appear to be technical or psychological interests in view. ("How much interest did you say he lost?" "What effect do you think their affair will have on the children?")
- Be positive. So very positive, in fact, that your listeners won't be able to stand it and will jump in to correct your saccharine tale with the latest slander.
- Be snide, funny, or sympathetic—just don't be judgmental. (God only knows the extent of your listeners' depravities!)
- Don't ask anything that will put others on alert. Never inquire after enemies, the competition, or your best friends. (If you're so close, why, don't they trust you?)

## You Don't Say!

While there's a natural tendency to tell friends what you have just read or heard about their ex-partners or pals, keep quiet. Most would rather forget those who have injured them—and still more those whom they have injured. It's not accidental that *martyr* comes from the Greek for "witness."

## Always Look Loyal

The best reputation is one for telling little while knowing much. If someone asks after intimates embroiled in a messy divorce, look him straight in the eye, smile, and say, "Well, John, why don't you ask them yourself?" Always look loyal. It's in your interest.

Never badmouth your spouse, stepchildren, patrons, or anyone else with whom you're thought intimate—however much you might hate them. Even after the most knock-down-drag-out divorces, train yourself not to say, "Did you hear what that bastard did?" but merely to shrug off questions with a smiling "Oh, sure, it was difficult."

As for your Trusted Few, there's no setback so big it can't be billed as "experience." No matter what, your friends are always doing "wonderfully": it looks so good on you.

## Protecting Sources

Enlightened self-interest also dictates loyalty to sources.

Feel free to name your source when such sourcing costs you nothing and shows your source off to advantage. The loftier your source, the more it lends your words authority. (As in "Roone Arledge says that show won't make it through the season.") But unless you're out to destroy the man, never cite *which* ABC vice-president called Arledge an "overbearing asshole."

While it's fine to "source drop" occasionally for effect (as in "Paloma Picasso says that when her father . . .") or even to share your source on some key item with intimates, the best rule of thumb on sourcing remains, *Don't.* It exposes your network, leaving them and you looking (sin of sins) like gossips.

# 20·Preemptive Tattling

> There are some occasions when a man must tell half
> his secret in order to conceal the rest.
>
> G. K. CHESTERTON, *All Things Considered*

---

## Who's on First?

> If the enemy is determined to fight, a field commander cannot
> avoid it; and so, to avoid battle at all costs really means to fight
> on the enemy's terms.
>
> MACHIAVELLI, *The Discourses*

It's psychological fact that we're more swayed by the first side of an argument we hear, unless forced to choose sides *immediately* after hearing the last one.

Disqualify critical witnesses when scandal threatens. While no man knows all his enemies *("Et tu, Brute?")*, most have a pretty good idea. If you know that someone is badmouthing you, warn friends to discount his story. Similarly, should you feud with one of your Trusted Few (to be avoided at all costs!), it's best to let others know you're not so close as you once were. (Don't *you* start spreading tales. But should *she* be indiscreet, you have already innoculated others against her stories.) While the discounting of detractors' credentials will be discussed more later, its usefulness *cannot* be overemphasized. Witness the Nixon team's handling of "mad" Martha Mitchell. She kept trying to tell us, and we kept refusing to listen.

## Getting the Jump

> United Nations, N.Y., Jan. 31—Jeanne J. Kirkpatrick says she has heard "whispers" from other delegations voicing "concern about Jewish influence" within the mission she heads here. . . . Both on the television program and in her conversation with a reporter, Mrs. Kirkpatrick declined to name the foreign delegations from which the "whispers" or "gossip" had originated.
>
> *The New York Times*, 1·31·83

The point of preemptive tattling is to show such will to fight that your opponents back off before the tangle. Thus, when pro-Arab delegates alleged undue Israeli influence to cow us, instead of ignoring such slander, Ambassador Kirkpatrick escalated the confrontation, putting the talkers on notice that while *she* wasn't intimidated, maybe *they* should be!

**The graceful exit.** Paloma Picasso was slated to buy manufacturer Irving Benson's million-dollar Central Park West triplex penthouse, but she *didn't*. "The French government said no and that was it," Benson told New York magazine, *Intelligencer*, referring to the socialist government's tight rules for letting money out of the country. But we *all* know, and Paloma herself said, "There are ways." Clearly, Picasso just didn't want the deal. But how clever of Benson to rush out the currency-regulations story that allowed him to advertise that tasteful Paloma had been willing to pay a cool million for his place, while obscuring the fact that she hadn't been so willing that she actually bought it!

## Dropped!

> Be in advance of all parting. . . .
>
> RAINER MARIA RILKE, *Sonnets to Orpheus*

The worst thing that could befall one socially is, of course, to be dropped; that is why one must take the dreadful news so very lightly, spreading word oneself—and so depriving one's "friends" of the satisfaction. Indeed, it almost forces them to counter your cries of "I've been cut! I've been dropped!" with a soothing, "No, no, you're wrong. I know Jade *likes* you." or "It wasn't that he cut you. I swear to God he just didn't *see* you!"

Similarly, when you've had some rough times and haven't heard from some "friends" in a while, steal the gossip's thunder. One divorcee, running into an old pal at Elaine's, greeted him with a jovial "Oh, hi, darling. People say that you've dropped me, but I always say, 'That's not true. He's simply waiting to see if I make it.' " Whether her fast-track friend still knew such a thing as shame or simply admired her guts, their friendship was promptly renewed and to this day, they're still seen supping together at Elaine's, dishing their mutual acquaintances.

**Paradise lost.** And then there's the trick of raising your status by pretending to have fallen from a former state of grace. ("I was dropped by Bill Paley." "Mick Jagger never calls anymore.") The countless society doctors who go around sulking each year after the Nobel Prizes are awarded also fall into this audacious group. Still, I consider the "paradise lost" pose to be a variety of leading with one's chin—and best avoided.

**A snitch in time.** Why wait to read about it in the papers, when you can influence what you read by feeding reporters items they would have picked up anyway? "I had a pretty important friend who was getting divorced—*real* messy—and everyone was starting to ask me, 'Is it true?' so I called him and said, 'Look, let me give this to Aileen [Suzy Knickerbocker].' He said, 'No, let me think about it.' But sometimes the only 'thinking' thing is *not to wait,*" Plugged In points out. "Sure enough, it's the main item on the next day's Page Six. Done in the meanest way! He called me, desperate for help, but by then of course it was too late."

## Qui s'accuse, s'excuse

> If you cannot get rid of the family skeleton, you may as well make it dance.
>
> GEORGE BERNARD SHAW

If Watergate proved anything, it was that stonewalling can sometimes be the best way to make the *worst* of a bad situation. While the actual French saying is "He who makes excuses himself accuses himself," when you think word will probably leak, my vote is for a preemptive *mea culpa*. New York's outspoken Mayor Ed Koch says outrageous things, which would do him even more damage did he not often steal his opponents' thunder by cracking, "Now wasn't that dumb? Can you believe I said that?"

**Straw men and beards.** Sometimes one might put out false news to obscure an even more damaging truth. *The Economist's* speculation on who will succeed sleepy Senator Hayakawa mentions Congressman Barry Goldwater, Jr., adding, "He is bedeviled by gossip, however, about the large number of women in his life." Funny, *that* isn't the talk around the capital!

Another time-honored preemptive tattling technique is to get on your own case. "You know, it's true, I haven't been much of a mother, always on the road working..." Of course the trial loses its terror when you take your own case in hand, because you never introduce the hanging evidence. After skimming lightly over some minor flaws, you quietly change hats and argue for the defense: "But maybe I wouldn't have traveled so much if Steve had ever worked—or hadn't played around with every *au pair* we ever hired..."

## Who's on the Skids?

> "What though the field be lost?/All is not lost...."
> Satan in Milton's *Paradise Lost*

So much of winning is attitude. Whether your trials are seen as setbacks or defeats is often a question of "How is he taking it?" (One just knew it was *sayonara* for the Shah when one heard reports that while revolution raged his Highness was holed up in the palace watching *Patton*.) Conversely, when Emperor Napoleon spent a livid cabinet meeting cursing out Talleyrand ("You're nothing but shit in a silk stocking") and our prince's only response was a cool "Isn't it a pity such a great man is so ill bred." One rightly suspected the minister would once again survive his master. Indeed, far from hiding news of his "disgrace," our prince raced from salon to salon recounting the emperor's tirade. Why would one of the world's wiliest gossips advertise such a scene? Best to give *his* claque the jump. It would all be out within the hour. Just so, when Louis XV stopped sleeping with Mme de Pompadour, instead of still pretending she was Royal Mistress, the clever marquise secured her spot as the king's lifelong friend by coolly breaking the "fatal" news herself. You can't always get what you want, but how you handle word of what you *do* get affects your prospects.

### Bedroom Farce

> Think you, if Laura had been Petrarch's wife,
> He would have written sonnets all his life?
>
> BYRON, *Don Juan*

Let us pause a moment to consider that most enduring source of scandal: not greed, fraud, or ambition, but rather one's own poor quest for fire. Here even Zeus cut a foolish figure. Politics may make for strange bedfellows, but not half so strange as the sort supplied by fancy! And oh, the deep-down torrent of recrimination that flows when one of the spellbound pair awakens from the idyll! The scenes! The spleen! And more amusing to one's friends, the gossip gleaned from dirty linen aired in public.

And breakups aren't the worst of it. There's always the even more awkward business of explaining our mate's failings *during*. "If you must needs marry, marry a fool," Hamlet advises, and many a wise man has. Talleyrand married a notoriously idiotic beauty, "stupid as a rose," he would smile when told of her latest blunders.

How to handle the usual, er, lapses? Why, by breaking your own bad news. When a Spanish prince known to be his wife's lover died, Talleyrand preempted the tattle of his "friends" by lamenting the late Spaniard himself. "Ah," he sighed in the best salons, "he always gave her such good advice. Now I have no way of knowing *whose* hands she'll fall into!" (Or, as Queen Alexandra murmured, seeing England's Edward VII on his deathbed, "Now, at last, I know where he is.")

To love is to make oneself ridiculous. If your remarks show that you grasp this, others will be less likely to make this observation for you in your absence.

## The Point of Poor-mouthing

> "You would not have seemed the devil then had you not seemed an angel to me on our first meeting."
>
> KLEIST, *Marquise of O*

The all-powerful must fear everyone, but if you don't pretend to be the world's fairest, you needn't get an ulcer each time a new belle bursts on the scene. Similarly, if we don't bill ourselves as a perfect pair, any turbulence is no big news and so less fatal.

Gossip is a game of expectations. Whatever is oversold soon sours. Claim only the turf you can defend. Far better to admit some liabilities up front, get them behind you, and start improving. (Studies show we prefer "bads" who become "good" to "goods" who simply stay "good," and we scorn "goods" gone wrong.) Even if you must be a hero, it's still best to start a heel.

Another point in poor-mouthing one's chances is to rally complacent troops. Front-running politicians who fear that their supporters won't bother to vote often start rumors that their rival is gaining.

**Trial balloons.** We sometimes leak stories to see how an act will "play" before we risk it. Thus a politician may leak word of his impending divorce and, if the polls aren't bad, go ahead with it. Similarly, a selection committee may leak leading candidates' names to smoke out any serious objections before appointment. When someone starting such a leak says, "I owe you an explanation," what he really means is "I want your reaction to my explanation."

**And now, the bad news.** Sometimes it's just not the championship season. What to do if you see a firing in your future? Be prepared—but above all, *prepare others* by preemptive tattling. Don't say anything against your boss, but do ask others about her recent "strangeness." "She was always so easy to work with before. Is she worried about her kids or just menopausal?" Leak like this and when you're forced out people will imagine you chose to leave because you found *her* "too difficult" to make the job worth it!

## The Defenders

> First, the heartbreaking word from Paris that it's all over for Valentino and his socially indefatigable Paris representative, Bettini Graziani. Bubbling Betts was uncharacteristically reticent on the matter, but admitted she's resigned. "There's no point in recriminations," she said. "I've left and it's over. I won't go back. Life is too short, and working relationships should always be harmonious."
>
> Privately, several of Bettina's friends confided to me they're outraged by her "mistreatment" by Val and business manager Giancarlo Giametti, following the arrival of a new Valentino exec, Sandra Elbilia, in Paris. "This woman is giving Bettina orders," said one chum. "And she didn't think it was fair. She feels she had no choice in the matter."
>
> W

When trouble is afoot, give your Trusted Few your story. (Nothing kills sisterhood more quickly than to have an *outsider* ask, "Tell me, why did Susan leave David?"—when your great chum Susie hadn't even told you she'd be leaving him!) Good business relationships can also fall prey to excessive discretion. ("I don't know how closely you imagine this is held, but I heard it from *my secretary.*") Keep breaking news from allies and you not only make them look like fools, you also lose their priceless help as your best defenders.

**From the horse's mouth.** While close friends expect our confidence, others are wary of unexpected confessions. ("Why is she telling *me?*" they wonder. "What's her angle?") Yet they feel no such resistance when hearing the very same hot news about us from our intimates.

## Come Clean with Your Defenders

Say you're just about to leave your mate, or quit the company you founded. Do give your Trusted Few advance word, but don't tell too much too fast, or those you're going to surprise may just *surprise you* by foiling your *fait accompli* before it happens! "Eighteen hours is all the advance word I ever give," one Machiavellian Ms. explains. "You're not only protecting *yourself*. Less notice also takes the heat off your friends. We tend to forget there are sometimes advantages to *not hearing* dangerous news. That's why when I have something hot, I always give friends the option of pretending they haven't heard it."

**The tale is told.** "If I were going to a close friend (one I knew wasn't going to burn me), I'd probably tell my tale with all the rancor, fury, and hatred in my heart—just *really* tell it. But if I were going to tell a columnist or a hostess (someone you can never seriously count on), I'd just try to get my major points in and then quit," one smart socialite explains. "Why clutter it with extras?"

"You don't draw the wagons into formation for every little thing, but for big news you should be *incredibly* selective," says another player. Even then it's not just a question of knowing *whom* to approach, but also *how*. Some give their personal best on the phone, while others prefer the quaint warmth of a face-to-face encounter.

But you can't always be sure. "You've just got to expect that no matter what you say, friends will do the natural thing and side with power," one lawyer shrugs. "If I know a friend basically disapproves of what I did, then I start right there and say, 'Look, I'm sorry, but I had no choice and now it's over. Will you help me?' "

"Maybe you tell just *two* people, but if you're counting on their help, you'd better damn well give them a full deck. Anything less is like lying to your lawyer," a sharp businessman counsels.

Who makes the best defenders? While any powerful, well-placed friend lends your story credibility, it's best to turn to your own sex in times of trial. "If Jack defends me—well, he really can't; his wife would kill him and it would make me look *worse*. But if Jill defends me—*how absolutely glorious!*" explains a powerful hostess. "You really need a woman defender."

**Dress rehearsal.** Part of the plus of preemptive tattling is that you get to pick who spreads your news. Some even give their Trusted Few a list. One socialite who was switching mates recalls: "My sister called and said, 'Don't you think it would be nice if you let Daddy know?' I allowed as how it would be. But first I called Claire and said, 'Okay, here are the people you have to call because I haven't the nerve! They're going to think I'm a fool, but *you* understand what I've lived through so you've got to be the one to explain it.'"

Once they've told your story, your defenders can cut back carping by saying, "Strange you should say that. She always speaks highly of you." Or: "If it's about Elaine again, let's drop it!" Or most effective of all: "I'm sorry to hear you say that. I really like her."

## Don't Leap to Leak!

#### WHO? ME? PANIC?

> For anyone who has a guilty conscience can easily be led to believe that people are talking about him.
>
> MACHIAVELLI, *The Discourses*

The many pluses of preemptive tattling notwithstanding, keep cool; don't leap to leak. You'd be amazed at the number of skeletons you *can* keep safely stacked away, so long as you don't invite inquiry with flagrant indiscretions. Besides, safe preemptive tattling requires artful advance work. If you've played a loner's game up to the crunch, suffer in silence. Even should you bet on your bad news not coming out and lose, there are still ways of surviving a bad story.

# 21 · When It's Already Out

> It's not the vice that ruins men, but the accusation.
> JOE ORTON, *Loot*

---

"You surprise me!" Ben Jonson's wife exclaimed, walking in on her husband *in flagrante delicto*.

"No, no, my dear. You weren't due back until four—it is *you* who have surprised *me!*" the playwrite reassured her. And, indeed, those of us caught with our pants down are often even more shocked than the unsuspecting (or perhaps not quite so unsuspecting) soul who finds us.

## Late Start

What do you do when your bad news is suddenly out all over town?

"It's much harder to sell your side when people think they have the facts already," says one whose pleasure is carefully plotted preemptive tattling. But even the best, brightest, and most beautiful monsters must sometimes play it as it lays. When your bad news is already out, don't despair. Deny it!

## No Defense Like Denial

> *Geraldine:* I'm not a patient. I'm telling the truth!
> *Dr. Rance:* It's much too late to tell the truth.
> JOE ORTON, *What the Butler Saw*

"When people are talking about your affairs, unless they have pictures—actual pictures *you see*—then you deny it," a rich divorcée advises. "And I think you can deny something in a way. Let's say my best friend comes to me and she says, 'Look, this is what I've heard,' and this is someone I love and trust. Well then, I would look her straight in the eye, pause, and say, 'I am going to deny that.' She gets the picture. The words may say one thing but the message is something else entirely."

And what if, horror of horrors, one of your Trusted Few turns and tattles?

"You still deny it. 'That's just sheer gossip! I don't know what her problem is.' That sort of thing," our serious socialite advises.

Even if people tell your mate?

"Absolutely! Deny it vehemently. Act aggressively aggrieved. Then he'll have something else to worry about, like whether you're going to scratch his eyes out," she counsels. "But when you're dealing with outsiders, keep it cool. Should a columnist call up, it's 'Darling, you I'd tell *anything*. It's just I don't know what you're talking about.'"

## You Can't Protest Too Much!

When Liz Smith let out that Steve and Eydie had split, Ms. Gorme got so riled she rented Carnegie Hall, where the durable duo then played to standing ovations. (Duly noted by the columnist, who wrote, "I was wrong and I'm glad.") Protesting too much? Guess not. Gossips love to get a rise. I've even heard a *New York Intelligencer* writer wax ecstatic about a power broker who promised to break his neck the next time "you make my wife cry" with premature separation notices. "What a guy! What a guy!" the awe-struck scribbler mumbled.

"A friend was in a restaurant when a man we both know came up to her and said, 'I understand you're having an affair with a much younger man. It's all over town.' Luckily her husband wasn't with her, but four friends were. She was so shocked she tried to make light of it. 'Oh,' she said, 'lucky me! Tell me, who is it?' Well, *that* was a mistake because the man then did the unspeakable and named the person!" A pal on the scene reports, "She had to let it slide that night but the next day, when she called him at the office, did she ever let him have it! 'How could you have so little respect for me! How could you have so little respect for my husband!' I would have given anything to have overheard *that* conversation! I rather doubt that left the Mouth much stomach for repeating his story."

What to do if plagued by accounting fraud or expense account scandals? Hire a shark, counter-sue, and stay on the job protesting innocence. (So what, if you finally get off on a technicality. Everyone around when the suit started will have long since retired.) Great are the uses of injured innocence. Never cop out unless . . .

### You're on Tape!

> I'm dumbfounded.
> 
> JFK aide Ted Sorensen on learning of JFK's tapes

> Let's not be naive. Taping takes place all the time, all over the world.
> 
> Former Nixon Press Secretary Ron Ziegler

Right you are, Ron. When ABC's Max Robinson accused his network of racism when speaking before a college group, that was his business. (If he wants to be a martyr, let him be a martyr.) But when he subsequently denied having made such remarks, that was just plain stupid. These days almost all group talks "on" or "off" the record are taped. (Official assurances are no insurance. Just ask the record companies about "bootlegged" performances.) Again, if you must tell tales out of school *please* not before an audience! While one witness is no witness, a crowd and a voice print make a clear case for indictment.

## "Misstating" Your Case

> Praised be all liars and all lies!
> BYRON, *Don Juan*

Oh, what a tangled web we weave when first we practice to succeed! Later, with practice, we get even better at it. What if the fact that you fled north to avoid the draft comes out years after your election to Congress billed as a veteran? Smart politicians in such a bind today would call a press conference and, while vigorously denying that they had "lied" (banish the word!), would admit to having "misspoken,"* going on (and on and on) to say that the issue was "trivial," indeed, "only an issue to those who want to obscure this campaign's real issues with petty carping." In other words, when scandal threatens, don't just deny the talk; attack the attackers!

## Look Who's Talking!

> Trevor: You're the one who made me violent. I was a pacifist before I met you.
> ALAN AYCKBOURN, *Bedroom Farce*

"Those whose conduct gives room for talk are always the first to attack their neighbors," Molière once observed, neglecting to add the coda, "with good reason." Casting stones creates a smashing diversion. Already under attack yourself? Don't fret. Affect the victim's sackcloth to show yourself more sinned against than sinning (and your critics scandal mongers). Defensive-aggressive remarks like "That's *just* a rumor" and "They've got a whisper

---

*This "misstatement" statement signals your will to fight and squashes speculation. (For why bother to speculate about what you've essentially admitted?)

campaign going against me" or "I'm being subjected to a trial by rumor" work well in complex scams that may take years to untangle finally—if ever. And speaking of your day in court, don't be shy about falling back on that "every man is innocent until proven guilty" cliché.

## The Genealogy of Morals and the Transfiguration of All Values

> "As for that," said Waldershare, "sensible men are all of the same religion." "And pray, what is that?" inquired the prince. "Sensible men never tell."
>
> BENJAMIN DISRAELI, *Endymion*

Indeed they don't (*tell,* that is, which is how they manage to continue imagining themselves to be of one mind). And so it is with sensible gossips. "Can you imagine anything so *tacky!*" we ask as our listeners shake their heads in agreement, such perfect sympathy part of the *entente cruelle* that binds the skillful gossip and his listener. Yet should we look closer, it's really not clear at all that we agree on what distinguishes *comme il faut* from a *faux pas.* While you, too, should strive to establish such instant complicity in your talk, should *you* come under attack, probe the speaker's often contradiction-ridden premises. Ours is *not* a consensus culture. By exposing value judgments implicit in the speaker's attacks, you narrow his support. Like the lover or the politician, the scandalmonger is also most compelling when most cryptic.

How to smoke critics out? Why, simply ask them to explain themselves. "What do you mean by 'difficult'?" you ask, your object to expose the attacker's "narrow-minded," "vague," or just generally shaky premises. What one critic pans as "inflexibility" his formerly sympathetic audience may soon (prompted by you) view as "artistic integrity."

**Beyond reason.** But why confine your queries to conscious grounds? With one smoothly insinuating, "Tell me, why does it *bother* you?" you shift the spotlight from your wicked deed to his "overreaction." If he's offended by your prodding, ask, "Where's all that anger coming from?" So much the bigger and better his "overreaction"!

## Guilty!—*with Excuses*

> Everything is relevant if its relevance can be invented.
>
> FRANK KERMODE, *The Sense of an Ending*

When absolutely cornered, you can still escape by pleading guilty —with excuses. There are three effective ways to do this.

First, you can simply 'fess up, and throw yourself on the mercy of the court. *Mea culpa.* You have seen the error of your ways. Tell all, hide nothing, and offer no defense beyond your impressive refusal to hide behind one. As Pope once observed, "A man should never be ashamed to own he has been in the wrong, which is but saying in other words, that he is wiser today than he was yesterday."

A slight variation on this technique is to admit one's guilt while refashioning the charge to one's advantage. Forging movieman Begelman and frolicsome former congressman Wayne Hays admitted to—not acts of fraud—but pitiable symptoms of stress and sickness.

## Guilty—*and How Ludicrous of You Even to Mention It!*

> On March 5th Lady Diana Cooper was fined 40 shillings for allowing her car to cause an obstruction outside a West End theater where she was attending a rehearsal. "We are not all lucky enough to have chauffeurs," remarked Lady Diana, said to have five convictions for similar offenses.
>
> BARROW, *Gossip*

What we shall call the "Adam Clayton Powell, Jr." defense, in honor of the late Harlem congressman, is as simple as it is effective. Simply say, "Yeah, I did it. So what?" *That* sure stops the whispers!

## Guilty—*and Proud of It!*

> Narrow minds may possibly have some reason to be ashamed
> . . . but he is a fool who is ashamed of being hanged, who is
> not weak enough to be ashamed of having deserved it.
> 
> HENRY FIELDING, *The History of the Life of Jonathan Wild the Great*

Instead of squashing scandal, you may want to fan the flames of infamy hoping to cash in on it! (At about $14.95 a shot—where there's a *Will, Blind Ambition* will find a way.) Call it "the wages of sin," but increasingly it seems that every devil's disciple has his day. The trick here is to appear just your average Joe, somehow cut in on the crime of the century, simply having done what came "naturally."

A cut above, genius pleads guilty with "I knew the world for the jungle it is" as its excuse.\* (After counseling duplicity, Machiavelli remarks, "If men were all good this rule would not be good, but since men are a sorry lot and will not keep their promises to you, you likewise need not keep yours to them.")

## Thumb Your Nose at Leaks

### YOU FEED THE PRESS

Newshounds are best controlled by careful feeding. Yet each new administration starts with a futile witch-hunt for "leakers." One can warn aides not to leak (and hope to cut the flow by five percent), but beyond this even Gestapo tactics like wiretapping fail. Witness Nixon's Watergate experiments. It's smarter to become a regular, "reliable" source yourself. You'll be amazed how fast the hard-pressed press will be seeing (and reporting) things

---

\*This special case of "guilty and proud of it" is also known as "guilty—to be absolved by history." (See the section after next, "Simply Above It.")

your way. Busy reporters think twice before attacking their own best sources.

Still, don't do a "Stockman." While power and the press make nice, *au fond,* theirs remains an adversarial relationship.

## Simply Above It

> I don't know Seymour Hersch, he's not a particular thorn in my side. . . . I've decided I'm not going to comment on that sort of article because it can go on forever.
> 
> HENRY KISSINGER, to Donahue, April 20, 1982

"Greatness once and forever has done with opinion," Emerson wrote in his essay "Heroism." While this is not of course strictly true, it is believed to be by nearly all, so simply not deigning to comment can be your best comment—especially when your acts were indefensible!

And one needn't always be curt. Many minor scandals simply blow over if you take them lightly. If someone says, "Aren't you involved with John?" laugh it off with, "Would it were true!" Get too haughtily defensive ("That's just gossip!") and you end up encouraging rumors.

# 22 · Character Assassination Explained: Or, How to Get Someone with Gossip

> How doth the little crocodile
> Improve his shining tail,
> And pour the waters of the Nile
> On every shining scale!
>
> How cheerily he seems to grin,
> How neatly spread his claws,
> And welcomes little fishes in,
> With gently shining jaws!
>
> LEWIS CARROLL,
> *Alice's Adventures in Wonderland*

"JUSTICE is as much a matter of fashion as charm is," our philosophical friend Pascal observed. And these days (men still being only what they always were) the times run from wicked to indifferent. And when the times are hard, how can our hearts be otherwise?

## The Open Attack

> Great wits may sometimes gloriously offend.
>
> POPE, *Essay on Criticism*

"What a wicked childhood I had with Princess Alice [Roosevelt Longworth]," Count de Chambrun, a seventy-five-year-old international lawyer and descendant of the Marquis de Lafayette fondly recalls for *W*. "She made everything fun and delicious and she could gossip like a great painter paints. She called me 'Bunny' and would arrive at our house and announce, 'Bunny, what news I have for you!' Then she'd regale me for hours with the sweetest tidbits from Washington." Alas, ours is a more precarious era. Only a few aging aristocrats recall the good bad old days when a fiery young Princess Alice could regale with tales of "good clean fun and bad family feeling," untainted by any motive save malice. Today it's only in sports and politics where, the rivalries more open, one needn't always pretend to speak out of disinterested concern for one's victim.

The open attack, shouting, or whispering campaign, is favored in sports where the sportsman's goal is to unnerve his opponent. Here Americans excel. Surely I needn't remind the reader of Connors' or McEnroe's great vituperative volleys?

Far less sportsmanlike smear tactics are used in politics where friends of the campaign may tip off reporters to alleged irregularities in the opponent's books or bedroom (allegations that are rarely laid to rest until *after* the votes are in and counted). Yet all such slander is not left to nameless aides. There sometimes emerges a figure so powerful, clever, or vicious that he indulges in the broadside. Talleyrand's response to Napoleon's question, "But isn't Mme de Stael at least a good friend?" is one such slam: "She is such a good friend she would throw all her acquaintances into the water for the pleasure of fishing them out." Lyndon Johnson's description of Gerald Ford as a man so stupid he couldn't "walk and chew gum at the same time" is another. The cleverer the line, the more likely it is that others will repeat it. But even less skilled attacks can be lethal.

## Open Season

> Sweet it is, when the mighty sea is lashed by furious winds, to look from the shore at the struggles of another.
>
> LUCRETIUS, *On the Nature of Things*

The world is just waiting to pounce on some people. Either their stock is too high, or they've stepped on toes, or both. Take the sad case of David Stockman, fearlessly wrestling the entire federal bureaucracy—and grabbing all the headlines—until he shoots himself in the foot, talking out of school. *Then* his colleagues do their best to see that the flesh wound proves fatal. How? They keep poking away at it, of course. The story was picked up like a cheerleader's pep cry. Insiders still couldn't get enough long after the entire country had tired of the naughty budget director's confession. Could young David have offended them *all?* No need: sharks aren't sticklers for due cause once there's blood in the water.

## Absent Friends

> How sweet the task to shield an absent friend! I ask but this of mine—*not* to defend.
>
> BYRON, *Don Juan*

When it comes to being "got" by gossip, we rarely know who fired the fatal dart. But if you're tracking down the source, start with your own good friends. Someone else brings up your name and, well, since they know so much (and familiarity, alas, often breeds envy or contempt), what can they do but share? "He's so wonderful. Isn't it tragic about his being fired?" "She's so pretty. I just wish she weren't a nymphomaniac."

## Making Inquiries

Often it's not your Trusted Few who do you in but those feigning familiarity, the better to torpedo you. Cleverer than "Oh, isn't it terribly sad that Jane has taken to drink" is putting your plant forward as a question: "What have you heard about poor Jane's drinking?" Or the still kinder cut, "People say Jane has become an alcoholic, but *I* just *won't* believe it!" Not very creative? Just plug any slam into this all-purpose formula: "Is it true $X$ did $Y$? I just like him so much I refuse to believe it!"

Another friendly way to get someone with gossip is to overpraise him in front of others. Say "I think David is the greatest writer of the decade" before a crowd of journalists; you won't be *able* to find an opening to stick your own knife in! Another good "get": relate what seems a nice bit of news ("Wasn't it nice of Dan to save Frank with that generous loan?") in front of Frank's worst enemy.

Other less-than-friendly "friendly" queries: "I've *never* seen her smoke like that! Was she always so nervous?" "Well, he was certainly flying tonight. What was he on?" Or simply, "Did Tim strike you as sort of funny?" Or even more innocently, "Does Tim have to take something for his back?" Or, "Isn't it wonderful that Jane and Jim got married! [pause] Whose idea was it? [pause] No, *really* . . . you don't think he's losing interest in her already?"

## Acid Asides: *In Passing*

> At every word a reputation dies.
>
> POPE, "Rape of the Lock"

The slur is often put to professional use by competitors who couch their slurs as warnings. While I was interviewing an agent who swore that *he* never badmouthed Eileen Ford ("and after all, *she* started it . . ."), a model just back from Europe came in. As the girl named each city where she had worked, the agent asked who had booked her—and greeted each name with a "careless" phrase maligning the rival. ("Be careful, the girls say he sometimes . . .") It came to him as naturally as breathing. While equally sharp operators wouldn't swallow such slurs, the girl's already oversized eyes grew wider.

**The jargon slur.** Any medical, movie, military, or Wall Street insider need only fall back on the jargon slur when dealing with outsiders. ("That's just the problem. Roger's fine for golf, but did you hear how he teed off on last week's triple bypass? Well . . ." Then begins a critique that, for all you know, might have been lifted from the *Annals of Internal Medicine*.) Jargon slurs impress most when delivered with a weary "why-must-I-always-be-the-one-who-has-to-tell-you-this" glance skyward.

**The throwaway.** "A friend of mine will often say, 'Yeah, but you know he uses a lot of drugs,'—throws it away, not 'My God, he's on everything but roller skates!' And because it's understated, I believe him," swears one beautiful monster. Other great throwaways: "I don't know. I haven't heard much. She must lead the bleakest little life." "Don't get upset by what he says. He's been sick for years. It's tragic." Throwaways work equally well whether they refer to loss of funds, friends, taste, or to a serious illness.

**Physical illness.** But wouldn't illness at least cause friendly concern? No siree, says one well-traveled up and comer. "You have to succeed, and being sick is not a successful thing." With the head of a big company, rumors of serious illness hang like Damocles' sword; even affecting the company's stock by impairing the chief executive's ability to make credible long-term commitments.

One can also casually imply others aren't good at their work: "I've heard there's trouble." "He may be moving soon." "I'm not so sure they're really that wild about him." "He's lucky to be there." "I don't think he'll be there much longer."

Offering a nonevent that prompts your listeners' contributions is another "innocent" aside:

*You:* He was there alone. I mean, he was just sort of sitting there alone.
*Listener:* That's right, I think I remember seeing him alone once at Mary's.
*You:* Every place I've seen him he's alone . . . It's funny, is he seeing *anyone* at all now?

Splits of all sorts provide endless nonmaterial from which to spin further such nonstories: "She really walked out on him

... I mean it was rather strange ... He just doesn't seem to be getting over it ... Tell me, what was the version *you* heard about her leaving?"

As far as slurs go, you can say almost anything; few ever really think about what they're hearing—or, for that matter, even about what they're reading. The strength of the slur is that it slips in, allowing the speaker to imply volumes without presenting a shred of evidence, or even making a clear charge so that the victim could at least attempt a defense.

## "Oh, But I Thought You Knew!"

One can always innocently disclose a "friend's" plans (or alleged plans) to his detriment by simply diving in as though you thought everybody else already knew: "After she sells the firm I thought we'd ..." Or you might ask a question introducing news that you pretend is already out. At the table you might ask, "I never *quite* got the story straight on Jane's row with her boss; what on earth was all the fuss about?"

"It's an excellent way to generate bad gossip!" enthuses Bella Donna. "Just start to mention something casually; then, when everybody goes, '*What?*' back way the hell off it, mumbling, 'But I thought *everybody* knew.'"

Bombshells are best introduced as minor corollaries of insignificant items. ("I don't think they'd dare sell the house in Connecticut—with his Senate run in the offing.")

Never present yourself as the source whenever you have the chance to make it appear you're merely repeating someone else's negative story.

Never volunteer dirt. Always make it seem that you're merely responding to questions.

## Now That You Mention It

Somebody else's darling Steve was fired and you'd like people to remember it. Play dumb. Make "innocent" remarks that resurrect the image of Steve as a loser. "I don't know why he would have taken that job. I would have preferred the one he left . . ." At that point the man next to you answers, "He didn't have a choice. It was either that or nothing, and what with his being so heavily in debt . . ." Merely mentioning divorce or drugs with relation to absent others makes your audience more aware of, and so likelier to discuss like problems of those present.

## Codes

"There are certain codes that we all know," one socialite declares. " 'He's very ambitious,' for instance. Or people say, 'She's not as pretty as she used to be.' Or 'She looks wonderful . . . *for her age.*' Or 'People say she has had a face-lift, but I don't believe it.' Or 'She seems a little thin; is something wrong?' Or 'At least she's a survivor.' "

Never mind that "he's very ambitious" could be said of almost anyone in your group. Fairness is rarely a speaker's major concern —*unless you force him to make it one.*

## Breaking the Code

The code's very vagueness makes it vulnerable to one easy (but rare) counterattack. If someone says of a friend, "She's very ambitious," just refuse to play, asking sweetly, "Why? Is that bad?" Or more pointedly, "Tell me, who isn't?"

Another variation: come back with the golden flip side of the slur. If someone downs a friend for ambition, you listen, smile, and say, "I think she has got guts." They say "tough" or "hard"; you say "smart" or "shrewd." They say "bitchy," you say "amusing." (This game of "paper/scissors" rarely goes past one round.) An even simpler way to clean up another's slurred speech is simply to say, "How *strange* you say that. I really like her." Your best proof against slander is always a (real) friend willing to speak up and be counted.

## Two Royal Saves

> "How do you like the Queen?" said the Cat in a low voice.
> "Not at all," said Alice, "she's so extremely—" Just then she noticed the Queen was close behind her listening: so she went on, "—likely to win, that it's hardly worthwhile finishing the game." The Queen smiled and passed on.
>
> LEWIS CARROLL, *Alice in Wonderland*

Clever Alice! Always try to be aware of who's around and stand ready to switch endings. A more wordly save was favored by Prince Talleyrand who, when surprised by the subject of his story would smile his sphinx-like smile and say, *"Ah—cher ami, nous venons de dire beaucoup de mal de vous!"* (Ah—dear friend, we were just saying terrible things about you!) Such sangfroid stunned his victim into silence.

## Killing Me Softly

> Damn with faint praise, assert with civil leer,
> And, without sneering, teach the rest to sneer.
>
> POPE, "Epistle to Dr. Arbuthnot"

It *is* a clever detractor indeed who talks one down by talking him up for qualities he doesn't possess (while ignoring those he might have). Similarly, if you answer my "How did you like the party?" with "Alice always has such good caterers," it makes you appear too nice to say what your remark implies: "Well, at least the food was edible." Or if a "friend" has done two noteworthy things, lavishly overpraise the minor one.

Damning with faint praise is more overtly hostile. The classic remark of this kind is Samuel Johnson's: "Worth seeing? Yes. But not worth *going* to see." Variations on this model can be pressed into frequent use, as can remarks along the "A" for effort but "D" for execution line, such as, "Well, at least you have to say he *tried*," or, "Yes, I saw the ballet, but remember he had just two days to rehearse those kids."

**Excuses, excuses.** When your partner points out a minor flaw, "defend" your victim with an excuse pointing up a major one. Thus, should someone say, "Damn, Harold is late again!" take poor Harold's part, explaining, "He really can't help himself, chronic lateness is part of the alcoholic personality."

**The backhanded compliment.** Then there is the backhanded compliment, so tried and true that it was already nicely described by Chaucer, who defined the backbiter as "the man who praises his neighbor but with wicked intent, for he always puts 'but' at the end and follows it with another of greater blame than the worth of the person." As in, "Isn't it brave how Cindy has put together what you could almost call a home above the A&P?" Or, "She has such a good sense of what becomes her; those flowing Halstons make her look almost slim." Chaucer also remarks on the ever-popular *odious comparison:* "If other men speak good of a man, the backbiter will say that he is very good but will point to someone else who is better still, thus disparaging he whom other men praise." Old ways are best ways.

## Who???

Don't *you* mention those whom you would rather see forgotten.

**The "no comment" comment.** The best put-downs are often those that imply the least interest. For example: "Hasn't Elaine's changed?" "I don't really know, I don't spend time there." Or, "What do you think of his style?" "I can't really say, I don't know his work." When Governor Carey hired a controversial new aide at his wife's urging, his aides were appalled. Asked about the appointment, Chief of Staff Bob Morgado simply said, "The governor has the authority to hire whomever he wishes." You can express boundless disdain with the right "no comment."

**The cryptic comment.** This is a seemingly kinder cut. "I don't want to say anything, but . . ." "She's changed." "Well, I guess he felt he needed the money." Or more openly," "Look, we were once friends, and I'd rather not say anything bad about her."

**The underhanded obit.** New York socialites interviewed all referred so consistently to Truman Capote in the past tense that

I began wondering whether I had missed the paper with his obituary.

**More obvious: the shrug-off.** "What do you think of Tom?" "Oh, he's nothing."

**Or the slip-in.** "Sue Mengers was wonderful in her day," one chatty producer told me. "Oh," said another socialite, "do they *still* see him? Well, I guess all sorts of unpleasant people need escorts."

**Can't put my finger on it.** "I don't know what it is about him. I keep *trying* to like him, but there's something that somehow bothers me." By this time your listener will have jumped in with specific ideas on just why it is your victim would rub anyone the wrong way. ("They're so hopelessly *nouveaux*. He's so grasping; she's so garish.")

## Blind-siding: *Meet the Press*

If you've got it in for someone riding high, you might want to tip off a journalist to some dirt you've just heard or created. (A politician might help a reporter out for months just to build the rapport that enables him to sell his story on an opponent: "Isn't it time *somebody* did a piece on Steve's links to the Libyans? I know lots of people who could help you.") Somebody getting your goat? Feed a blind item to a columnist who doesn't bother to check. After all, why ruin a perfectly good story?

Then there's the standard "blind-sider." Has there ever been a profile published in the *Washington Post*'s Style section without the obligatory green-eyed monsters' carping? "He has a reputation as a young guy on the make," says a White House aide. "He's been all over the lot," complains another. (The foregoing comments come from a piece on White House deputy chief of staff Richard Darman, but could just as easily have been lifted from any power "profile" printed in the past three decades.) While blind-siding* is standard journalistic fare, *Washington*

---

*\*A modest proposal:* I have no doubt that reporters never make up quotes but always sally forth to get yet another brace of aides to backstab their fellows. Still this process seems a bit redundant and outdated. Why not collect all such blind-siders once and for all, and use them as the data base for a computer program called Central Swipe

*Post* Style reporters pour it on as freely as Italian cooks ladle tomato sauce.

## You Don't Say!

"It isn't bad enough that Elizabeth Taylor had to put up with Kitty Kelley's new book about her. Now poor Liz has to tolerate Kitty's wisecracks as the writer sashays around the country plugging the book...." Thus begins one "Page Six" column that, after dishing Kelley for tattling on Liz, goes on to repeat the same "nasty" stories.

"Oh, I say, it was just awful!" swears one former member of Vice-President Rockefeller's staff. "The girl was too tacky for words. She was on the staff and had nothing to do but... So she was just dying of boredom. You might almost feel sorry for her, if she hadn't asked for it. Absolutely shameless, the way she first came on to him—and the things she said! I kept saying, 'Stop! Don't tell me. I still have to work with the poor man,' but she would just go on in the most excruciating detail... You know how it is with men that age... Though he kept her a virtual hostage, all he wanted..."

Poor Rocky! If you've been privy to the inside scoop on sensational material of questionable taste, the smartest course is to whet your listener's appetite ("Yes, I talked to her after that night"), then beg off ("No, I can't repeat it, it's just *too awful*"). "I'll be damned if I'm going to be the one putting *that* rumor out on the street!" one gossip regularly declares after telling a group the foulest stories.

---

instead. A few weeks after the Inaugural, standardized forms would be passed out and each potential source (from personal secretary to secretary of state) would be asked to check "not-for-attribution" remarks about colleagues with #2 lead pencils. For example: "(a) He wants to be Secretary of State; (b) He's all over the lot; (c) He was changed after 'Nam; (d) We go back a long way—I knew him when he was a liberal." To ensure against respondents accidentally being held responsible for their remarks, informers needn't give their names but should offer an identifying tag (such as "one influential White House aide" or "one astute inside observer"). As in the past, such labels will inevitably be inflated.

## Legitimate Concern

> I had rather have this tongue cut from my mouth than it should do offense to Michael Cassio, yet I persuade myself to speak the truth.
>
> <div align="right">Iago framing Cassio in Shakespeare's <i>Othello</i></div>

Like "honest Iago's" handiwork, character assassination often masquerades as legitimate concern. Casting directors, sales managers, personnel officers, editors, all manner of managers, work-review committees, and producers have a real professional interest in what Johnny can deliver on the job—which can mean they also need to know what he's into after hours. (Why, for instance, do some say Johnny's command of the camera has been getting shaky?)

"I gossip with other casting directors a lot," says one hot West Coast casting director. Since the usual stigma against passing judgments is dissolved in such working sessions, the slurs rain faster than at haute biche cocktails—and do immeasurably more damage.

"Say someone suggests we cast June," the casting director explains. "If I think she's a bitch I might say, 'Wonderful, is she out of the hospital yet?' Or, 'Oh, is she working again?' implying she's alcoholic or on drugs. Or, more creatively, 'Isn't she a bit *butch* for that?' Another good one I heard at a meeting yesterday was, 'He's great—*before* lunch.' You have to remember, we've all got our asses on the line. Casting isn't a rational process. I know when I hear, 'Oh, he's great *before* lunch' that maybe he was only seen drunk once at some party, but if I haven't the time to delve into it (I haven't *any* time), I just can't afford to risk it."

Movie people are so big on keeping book that at Paramount, at least, there's allegedly a "white" list of "enemies" with whom the studio won't work. Whether or not this list really does exist, "he's on the list" is a shorthand slur used in a range of industries.

Codes obviously vary from business to business and from group to group. Homosexuals might put down bisexuals with a disdainful "He'll fuck *anything* that walks!" while a predominantly bisexual group might trash both straights and gays for their "inflexibility." But whatever the group's mores, the worst reputation to have is that of a shameless user given to borrowing money, inviting oneself, or otherwise putting people on the spot by asking favors. "I despise the honesty of beggars," Rimbaud wrote, speaking for many.

## More Oral Sadistic Phrases

> It is well, if when a man comes to die, he has nothing heavier on his conscience than having been a little rough in conversations.
>
> EDMUND BURKE

**What becomes a legend most?** If you have a knack for knowing, you might consider spinning apocryphal tales. Did Nero *really* fiddle while Rome burned? Did Marie Antoinette announce, "Let them eat cake"? Historians say no, but their enemies were clever enough to spread stories that, while not literally true, were so right on target, they became legend.

**Comparisons are odious.** If you've no specific charges, but just know what you hate, consider the odious comparison. Transexual similes are particularly apt as they obscure important non-sexual differences while making your victim appear even more ridiculous. If, for example, your "friend" is pushy, *nouveau*, and obnoxious, laughingly suggest, "I've begun to think of him as a male Evangeline Gouletas-Carey."

**A friend indeed.** A great way to start bad rumors is to appear to be "forced" into it out of your greater love for your victim's alleged intended victim (i.e., the listener). Thus you present yourself as willing to make the ultimate sacrifice of allowing your listener to think you a "gossip" in order to spare him a nasty experience. "I know it's none of my business, but just for the sake of my own conscience I had to make sure, before you hired David, that you knew . . ."

**Easy rider.** One of the easiest ways to make a bad story more credible is to slip it in right after honestly answering another question. Your item then acquires credibility by association.

**Straight-shooter.** Those with a reputation for saying the hard things and "telling it like it is" frequently get away with telling it like it really isn't. Such speakers should take the "I am not cruel only untruthful" stance and appear to dish without fear or favor. Prefacing your remarks with phrases like "I don't know how well you know him but..." help to heighten the illusion that your first concern is always truth and not your listener's good opinion.

**The sentence.** If I say, "I don't think Jim is working out," that's just one more opinion, but if the man with hire/fire power over Jim says, "He tried to change, but let's face it, he's failing," that's news. Some business types tend to be blunt. One grows accustomed to hearing "fail" used as a verb describing something besides unsatisfactory schoolwork. "She's just not cutting it," "She has nothing to offer," "He isn't serious," and "Let's face it; he's finished" are pretty damning when said by those in power.

**Common knowledge.** "How do you know?" one reporter asked me over drinks. "Why, darling, I'm amazed at your ignorance," I replied. "Absolutely everyone who's anyone has known that forever!" Much to my surprise, the journalist turned crimson and stammered, "I admit it was a stupid thing to ask," when of course it wasn't a stupid question at all—but I was hardly going to admit that! Such phrases as "Oh, it's common knowledge," "Haven't you heard?" and "Oh, that again!" also vouch for your "evidence."

**Don't tell anyone, but—** One of the most effective ways to get someone with gossip is to share your story as a secret. Once, when I was doing an article involving some Soviet émigrés, another journalist told me that the FBI had asked him about one of the émigrés and implied they believed the man was a KGB agent, *but* they told the journalist not to tell. This journalist then told me, of course, while telling me not to tell, making it hard for me to go back to the FBI and ask, "What gives on this guy? What's the basis for your suspicion?"

All of which points up a great way to start a rumor. If that journalist told me, he probably told ten others. If the FBI told him, they also told ten others who told ten others, etc. The "don't tell anyone" technique works for office and social intrigues as well as for espionage. The key is to know what people are primed to believe; then, the murkier the situation, the greater your leverage. So if you want to safely "get" someone, start your talk with a heartfelt "Swear you won't tell anyone? This was told to me in confidence..."

## Creating a Character

> *Iago:* She did deceive her father, marrying you; and when she seemed to shake and fear your looks, she loved them most.
> *Othello:* And so she did.
> *Iago:* Why, go to them!
>
> SHAKESPEARE, *Othello*

It has been ever thus. We like to think of "character" as a fairly straightforward, fixed quantity; that's why we call "character" witnesses to the bar. He is a "liar"; she is a "saint." And of course, since we all know that "birds of a feather flock together," the assertion of acquaintance instantly blossoms into a "proof" of shared guilt.

The facts, of course, aren't half so simple. People are rarely entirely good, greedy, or bad—but isn't it reassuring to think so? The smart gossip need but sketch in a few deft lines for his listener to leap to the conclusion: "Archfiend," "True Lady," "Genius," or "Child Molester."

And while you're up to no good, steal a page from the agitprop bible of the "Moral Majority." Remember, there's no stone like the first stone, carrying with it, as it does, the presumption of *the thrower's own innocence.*

## The Smear: *Call Me Irresponsible* . . .

> Our political tradition sets great store by the generalized symbol of evil. This is the wrongdoer whose wrongdoing will be taken by the public to be the secret propensity of a whole community or class. . . . To uncover an evil man among the friends of one's foes has long been a recognized method of advancing one's political fortunes . . . and adds to the firmness with which evil is attributed to all who share his way of life. . . .
>
> J. K. GALBRAITH, *The Great Crash*

The smear is a dirtier business than the slur. While the slur is dropped in bitchy passing, the smear is often part of a holy war. (Man is never so inhuman as when serving a "higher" purpose.) Take the recent case of the much-maligned, hotly defended Jacobo Timmerman, an Argentine journalist who spent two and a half years as a prisoner of the Argentine junta. Released in 1979, his short memoir *Prisoner Without a Name, Cell Without a Number* and his pro–"human rights" speeches made him adored by liberals and detested by conservatives who started searching for ways to discredit him. When the need to smear is strong, can the charges themselves be far behind? "Give us a man and we'll make a case," is not the KGB's motto for nothing!

When Timmerman accused the Argentinian regime of anti-Semitism, conservatives such as Irving Kristol blasted him for speaking out and thereby exacerbating what the Neo-cons had just denied was a problem. The Neo-cons also hit Timmerman for his (alleged) involvement with missing (alleged) terrorist financier David Graiver. A serious charge. The evidence? Nothing beyond vague claims of the same "authorities" who, though they held Timmerman for years, never had enough of a case to press charges in their own kangaroo courts!

"Not to worry," say Timmerman's critics. "Maybe we can't prove he's a guerrila—but he's certainly a fraud. If he cares so much for human rights, why didn't he protest the treatment of 15,000 of his countrymen who 'disappeared' earlier?" And there the matter rested. (After all, Timmerman's critics could hardly be expected to point up their own pretzel logic, to wit, that if Timmerman's timid liberalism got him imprisoned, any more outspoken protest would killed him)

There are some men who stand firmly by their principles in the face of death, but Sakharovs are scarce. Showing that a man is not a saint merely proves him human, not the devil. But we don't think. Instead, we hear or read some slander and assume, "Well, they wouldn't print that if it weren't true."

**There's no defense like a good offense.** Whenever you come under attack and haven't a leg to stand on, charge! Mount a vigorous smear campaign against your attacker. The critical spotlight then shifts from the irrefutable charges against you to those hurled against your critic. And even if your "honest mistake" is exposed, you're ahead of the game. Few who read your stinging headline will see the morrow's minute "correction."

## Persuasion

> Truths are illusions about which one has forgotten that this is what they are. . . . [To] be truthful means using the customary metaphors . . . in society, to lie according to fixed conventions.
>
> NIETZSCHE, *On Truth and Lie* (posthumously published fragment)

In order to convince, we must create a case that appeals to popular conceptions of "proof," conforming to (often misleading) clichés rather than to messy reality. "That doesn't sound right" really means not that it can't be true, but rather, "You have screwed up on form" (perhaps by changing your story slightly when the ritual of "telling the truth" requires verbatim repetition—actually more a test of memory).

While better-educated people think themselves more "skeptical," this doesn't make them less immune to persuasion. It's just a question of changing fashions in evidence. While a priest may fail to convince you that "this rock will kill you," a scientist need only murmur "radioactive" to spur a stampede away. The key is pitching your "proof" to appeal to your audience's prejudices.

## Audience as Accomplice: *They'll Meet You Halfway*

> Calumny is like counterfeit money: many people who would
> not coin it, circulate it without qualms.
>
> DIANE DE POITIERS

We can understand why interested parties might slander each other more easily than we can see why "innocent" bystanders are so often eager to spread scandal. But even "noncombatants" develop a psychological stake in spreading the story. Many like to present themselves as a source of "inside" news because it gives them power over others.

Social psychologists speak of the "comfort" of sharing an emotionally charged rumor. It's almost as if, caught in certain situations, most people would rather settle for a wrong answer than suffer the angst of keeping an open mind. This is why rumors proliferate when the demand for "hard" news outpaces the supply. Not surprisingly, studies show that those with a low tolerance for ambiguity (ethnocentric and authoritarian personalities) will buy (and spread) rumors that more laid back souls pass by.

## In for a Dime, in for a Dollar

> When the press learned of the wire taps on newsmen and
> White House staffers, for example, and flat denials failed, it
> was claimed that it was a national security matter. I'm sure
> many people believed that the tapes were for national security;
> they weren't. That was concocted as a justification after the fact.
> But when they said it, you understand, they really *believed it.*
>
> JOHN DEAN, *Playboy* interview

Complicity grows on you. Much like the salesman who's halfway home with a foot in the door, crack gossips know that they can sell a reluctant audience a farfetched tale by *getting their listeners to participate in the telling.* Say you are joined by a third party. You might ask your original listener to recount the story "so far." Or you might tell something so hot your listener would repeat it whether he believed it or not. People often come to *truly believe* what they initially thought false but "too good not to repeat." What happens?

The answer is offered by the theory of "cognitive dissonance." In brief, Jane sees herself as a "nice" person. Jane hears a juicy story about her friend Dick that she doesn't really believe but just *has* to tell. Then Jane begins to experience cognitive dissonance: "If I'm such a nice person," she wonders, "why did I repeat that wretched lie about Dick and Spot?" Ergo: "Maybe I'm not really as nice as I'd like to think . . ." Here Jane jumps up and starts anxious pacing. "Or *maybe*," her subconscious thoughtfully suggests, "just maybe the story is true after all." In fact, it's a logical necessity: since nice people don't spread lies and I'm a nice person, the story must be true. *Voilà!* Saying is believing. Lying produces an attitude change in the liar. Ironically, the greater the cognitive dissonance the lie produces (that is, the higher Jane's initial self-esteem, the more damaging the lie, and the smaller the external justification), the more likely Jane is to start truly believing her own false story. Poor Dick! Poor Spot! "Well," Jane's listeners say to themselves, "the story must be true. After all, Jane has no motive for lying about those two."

Exactly!

## Blaming the Victim

> He must be wicked to deserve such pain.
>
> ROBERT BROWNING, "Childe Roland to the Dark Tower Came"

Some of the most malicious rumors are fueled by our desire to see the world as a just place. Again, somewhat paradoxically, the higher our self-esteem, the more we're interested in this illusion. If something terrible is said about someone whose stock is down, we'll tend to endorse the rumor; it reassures us that life isn't unfair. The victim "had it coming."

Rumors are often a sort of public rationalization. During riots, rumors of police beating children and of rioters sniping at cops often spring up to make it easier for each side to justify assaulting the other. One of the things that Khrushchev remembers with a straight face is that after Beria's arrest "we discovered" that the former secret police chief had raped over a hundred seventh-graders! What a lively senior citizen! How convenient! "The last king/ of a fallen dynasty/ is seldom well spoken of," observed Auden.

# 23 · The Whole Truth and Several Usefull Variations

*All true is simple—is that not doubly a lie?*
NIETZSCHE, *Twilight of the Idols*

REPEATING an inaccurate story and attributing it to an enemy is, of course, a wicked lie. But then, what is Truth, especially when it comes to gossip? (Is Beauty truth? Truth beauty? Then why does "the naked truth" inspire not sighs but shudders?) Beats me. Whatever its value for the soul, extreme honesty is most disruptive, and total candor a vice forgiven only the very young, the vastly old, and the ridiculously wealthy. For the rest, society requires that we master the fine art of shading. Or as Disraeli observed, "A gentleman is one who knows when to tell the truth and when not to."

## Truth and Consequences

> A powerful enigma is a dense one, so that, provided certain precautions are taken, the more signs there are, the more the "truth" will be obscured.
>
> BARTHES, *SZ*

Never lie to yourself—much. Unless you own up to who you really are, you'll never know what faults you should be hiding.

Don't lie about your past; a masterful vagueness is usually enough to start others spinning stories you need neither confirm nor deny. Above all, be careful with specifics. Gone are the days when a presidential hopeful could pretend to have attended London School of Economics, then take the credit (and a Pulitzer) for books written by others. The sort of fibs that helped get JFK the nomination got New York senatorial hopeful Bruce Caputo dropped from the ticket (Bruce claimed to have served as a draftee when he hadn't). Get caught in a lie about your credentials and with one stroke you've destroyed your credibility on *everything*.

More subjective personals offer room for hedging. You can call those eight deadly dull years with your late wife "peaceful."

Once you tell your story, be consistent. If you can't keep track of every fib, cut back on drinking, pills, or lying.

Never lie to your personal lawyer.

Never lie to your doctor of last resort.

Never lie to a VIP from whom you're asking a favor. Master gamesmen tend to check out stories, and whatever their own dishonesties, they despise being lied to. So don't do it. Especially since such favors are done on the *quid pro quo*, not the merit, system, anyway.

Favors are a touchy business. If you're passing news along to pick up points, make extra sure it's accurate.

## As You Like It

> A mixture of the lie doth ever add pleasure.
> BACON, "Of Truth," *Essays*

If you set your stories up right, you can often take easy, no-risk liberties with the truth. Once you've tagged a tale "something I heard the other day," you're free to wing it.

Exploit your ignorance. Have it your way when you're not the expert. Say, for example, that an enemy's program has been moved from 8:00 P.M. to a better, later hour. To zap her, just say,

"Poor Louise. Too bad they've bumped her back to that awful eleven-thirty slot!" Your listener will have long since forgotten the details of your talk should he ever discover your "mistake." (Undoubtedly an innocent one. After all, why should *you* know about radio?) What he *will* retain is the misimpression that your poor "friend" Louise is slipping.

## The Art of the Possible

> I have always felt that the art of telling a story consists in so stimulating the listener's imagination that he drowns himself in his own reveries. . . .
>
> HENRY MILLER, *The Colossus of Maroussi*

The best gossip has never been a slave to fact. Rather, it reflects the whole shimmering spectrum of human means, motives, insecurities, and obsessions. Still, much like the novelist, politician, or economist, the good gossip often uses actual events as inspiration for his story. (As in the above example, when the "true" scheduling shift of the program lent credence to a complete misrepresentation of this fact's actual significance.) While such touch-ups are safe and easy, eschew the big lie. It instantly commits you to a web of supporting lies only a Proustian obsessive could maintain. Similarly, don't overreach or overembellish.

"New" stories should always be internally consistent. The most repeatable "new" stories are tight, clear, eminently repeatable, credibly in-character, and *absolutely uncheckable*.

"New" stories are best presented to several different storymongers almost immediately. When they hear a story from more than one source, most people never check back but immediately think, "Ah, a second source, this must be true," much like a lazy reporter.

Stories gain credibility if you maneuver others into asking for them: "I saw the oddest couple out lunching. I can't believe how careless people are becoming nowadays. Remember last year when we . . ." "But who was it?" interrupts your listener.

If your listener approached you for news, you probably couldn't *make* him disbelieve you. So fib all you want, after throwing in a disclaimer. Suppose Paula, the mad, monied divorcée, is a chum of yours. If asked the source of Paula's money, you may answer, "All from her ex? No, if I'm not wrong [as you intentionally are!], her family had money. Didn't she meet Paul after getting booted out of Vassar?" Indeed, the best false story is pure suggestion. How much greater the ease (and less the risk) when you imply false volumes with one truly misleading remark: "Nan said she ran into John and Steve in the Village the other night and . . . Well, she thought . . ." There, the story is off and running.

## Where There's Smoke . . .

> Gossip is mischievous, light, and easy to raise, but grievous to bear and hard to get rid of. No gossip ever dies away entirely if many people voice it: it too is a kind of divinity.
>
> HESIOD, *Works and Days*

"Isn't there something funny going on with the Fischer partnership?" "I hear John has almost lost his touch and is on the way out . . ." "Poor Mary looked so genuinely downcast at the funeral. Hasn't anyone told her Carl was sleeping with his secretary? Didn't he leave that dreadful girl a pile of money? . . . *Nothing?* Well, that's how men are . . . There you have it!"

There indeed (almost indelibly), you do have it. Once a rumor starts, despite all evidence to the contrary, it can sometimes not only follow you to your grave, but can survive you, given a life of its own by the many who have heard, adopted, and repeated the story.

"But surely, where there's smoke, there's fire?" the gentle reader asks.

"Only up to a point," the author answers. While Rumor lives in the same neighborhood as Truth, the pair often take separate apartments. Flames may not be smoldering quite where you think. A few people murmuring that you've lost your deal-making magic doesn't mean it's necessarily true. But if most feel it sounds right enough to repeat, your marketplace luster is surely tarnished. Besides, if they aren't afraid to whisper, you must be losing your grip on *something*.

## Pretty Lies: *Just Tell Me What I Want You to Tell Me*

> This is the sublime and refined point of felicity, called the possession of being well deceived.
>
> JONATHAN SWIFT, *A Tale of a Tub*

"Are you going to believe what you see, or are you going to believe what I tell you?" one sharp agent asked his fading lady when she burst in on him while he was uncovering fresh talent. Since he was not just her leading man but also her meal ticket, the fading lady gratefully snatched up even this feeble face-saver. It was yet another case of *needing* is *believing*. And so it is with gossip. Your credibility lies as much in how much your listener wants to believe your story as in how well you tell it.

The relevant truth in rumor is not whether what was repeated literally occurred, but the slant given events when a story is picked up and repeated.

## Never Repeat the Wrong Truth

> In the winter gloom of Moscow, Boris the Gypsy, a minor performer for the Bolshoi Ballet, was practically incandescent. He wore open sports shirts and a diamond-encrusted pendant; he drove a green Mercedes. But the lights dimmed on Boris a month ago when police nabbed him with a trove of hot diamonds . . . and the scandal took an even darker turn when it turned out that Galina Churbanova, the daughter of Leonid Brezhnev, was an old friend of Boris. . . . Some gossips said Boris had implicated Galina in the scandal. . . . but the speed with which the rumors spread led some to speculate that they

had been planted to hurt Brezhnev. "The rumors may be more important than the reality behind the rumors," said one Western diplomat. A seasoned Muscovite put it more bluntly: "I see in this a sign of a struggle for power."

*Newsweek,* "A Three-Ring Scandal," March 8, 1982

Only saints, fools, and ambitious young journalists speak ill of the powerful in anything above a whisper. "What is truth?" jesting Pilate asked. People don't necessarily believe the lies they repeat any more than they may doubt the inconvenient truths they bury. It's just that, in the fast lane at least, news you repeat had better be useful. "Right" or "wrong," your gossip should promote you and yours (but not so wildly that it threatens the more powerful). Far from loose talk, gossip is the social currency with which we gamble, and the chips by which we mark each player's success or failure.

# 24·Surviving a Bad Story

> For forty years I was the most morally discredited man in Europe and yet I was always either all-powerful or just about to come back into power.
>
> TALLEYRAND

NOTHING lost, it seems, save honor. Should scandal strike, "just hang out and hang on," one bi-coastal beauty counsels, adding, "in style." So what if the Securities and Exchange Commission holds that you misled stockholders? So what if you stabbed your second wife, or you're being sued for rooting your bestseller in another's unsung novel? Not to worry, darling, you're still the star. Just settle quietly out of court and there'll be no fuss beyond the usual sniping.

"There are no 'morals' to transgress, just a rap to beat," explains one corporate counsel. "This is the *age* of gossip. So many new scandals hit people each day, they can't possibly bear *yours* in mind."

"Just look at what the people we know have survived. If it hits the papers and gets messy, so what? There'll be a new column the next day about someone else. Look at Barbara Walters. You could say she has failed because she's no longer anchor. But she has survived . . . because she hung in and made it seem as if she just changed rather than failed. And so she really hasn't failed (though to hear Mike Wallace tell it, she has failed). She still pulls audiences and has power."

Why do some people just collapse and others move on to the

next round? "It's having a sense of yourself *and* the ability to take it," says one who is also no slouch at dishing it out, "because I guarantee if you're visible, you'll be a target for gossips!"

## Self-reliance

> You have too much respect for the world:
> They lose it that do buy it with much care.
>
> SHAKESPEARE, *Merchant of Venice*

When Emperor Fabius Maximus was told, "The people are mocking you," he retorted, "But I am not mocked," meaning, the usually terse Tacitus tells us, "The only people who really suffer ridicule are those who allow it to influence them and are put out by it." Brave words! Yet one wonders whether Billie Jean King, too, sees surviving a bad story as a question of mind over masses. Not yet, perhaps, but keep the faith. When martyrdom comes, can beatification be far behind? "Greatness always appeals to the future," Emerson exhorts. *Any* sort of greatness. Sir Max Beerbohm quipped: "Ordinary saints grow faint to posterity, whilst quite ordinary sinners pass vividly down through the ages."

So you're the scandal of the week: the IRS is on your back, the SEC is on your case, rumor has it your contract won't be renewed, and word that you've just been dumped by your husband, dropped by your love, and cut dead by "polite" society is splashed all across the papers. What to do? Why, darling, there's just one thing someone in your position *can* do. (No, no, not *that*. Unhand that wrist!) Remember, life is like skiing: part of the sport is surviving the falls. Folks have said every fool thing about this vale of tears, except that it was easy.

But it can be *easier*. Since both you and the talk are here to stay, spare yourself unnecessary bumps by being a smart gossip. Keep your eyes open, your ears peeled, your tongue on a tight leash, and your mind set on "skeptical." Always lend an ear, even to what they're saying about you. Don't take the talk too much to heart; don't hope to control it; but do give a vigorous go

## 224 EXPERT / Hard-Core Gossip Gamesmanship

at influencing it by all and any means presented in this primer.

"Of those things that terminate in human life, the world is the proper judge: to despise its sentence, if it were possible, is not just; and if it were just," sensible Sam Johnson observed, "is not possible." So, dive into the fray, but dig the paradox: you can only win at worldly games like gossip if you're "philosophical" about it. For the rest, leave it to heaven. May you have your will with Fortune. May you lose that last ten pounds. May true love find you, yet not linger so you die of boredom. And above all, may this guide help you not just survive, but *conquer*.